Money M
Change Your Habits, Change Your Life

The Foundations of a Prosperous Mindset

Understanding Your Relationship with Money

Our relationship with money is complex and multifaceted. It is shaped by our upbringing, culture, experiences, and beliefs. Understanding our relationship with money is essential for developing a prosperous money mindset and transforming our financial habits. In this book, we will explore how to understand your relationship with money and how to transform it to achieve greater financial success and fulfillment.

1. Your Money Story

Our relationship with money is shaped by our money story, which is the narrative we tell ourselves about money. Our money story is influenced by our upbringing, culture, experiences, and beliefs. It can be positive or negative, and it can affect our financial habits and mindset. Understanding our money story is essential for transforming our relationship with money.

2. Money Mindset

Our money mindset is the set of beliefs, attitudes, and emotions we have towards money. It is shaped by our money story and can affect our financial habits and decisions. A prosperous money mindset is characterized by abundance, gratitude, self-worth, mindfulness, purpose, generosity, and faith. Understanding our money mindset is essential for transforming our relationship with money and achieving greater financial success and fulfillment.

3. Money Habits

Our money habits are the actions we take with our money. They are influenced by our money mindset and can affect our financial well-being. Good money habits include budgeting, saving, investing, and giving. Bad money habits include overspending, debt, and financial procrastination. Understanding our money habits is essential for transforming our relationship with money and achieving greater financial success and fulfillment.

4. Money Beliefs

Our money beliefs are the deep-seated assumptions and attitudes we have towards money. They are shaped by our money story and can affect our financial habits and mindset. Common money beliefs include "money is the root of all evil," "money can't buy happiness," and "money is scarce." These beliefs can limit our financial potential and create negative emotions towards money. Understanding our money beliefs is essential for transforming our relationship with money and achieving greater financial success and fulfillment.

5. Transforming Your Relationship with Money

Transforming your relationship with money requires awareness, intention, and effort. Here are some tips for transforming your relationship with money:

- Identify your money story: Reflect on your upbringing, culture, experiences, and beliefs to understand how they have shaped your relationship with money.
- Develop a prosperous money mindset: Cultivate abundance, gratitude, self-worth, mindfulness, purpose, generosity, and faith to transform your money mindset.
- Build good money habits: Budget, save, invest, and give to improve your financial well-being.
- Challenge your money beliefs: Identify and challenge your limiting money beliefs to transform your relationship with money.
- Seek support: Seek support from a financial coach, therapist, or mentor to help you transform your relationship with money.

The Connection Between Mindset and Wealth

Our mindset is a powerful tool that can either help us achieve wealth and success or hold us back from reaching our financial goals. In this chapter, we will explore the connection between mindset and wealth, and how we can develop a prosperous mindset that supports our financial abundance.

1. The Power of the Mind

Our mind is a powerful tool that can shape our reality. Our thoughts, beliefs, and attitudes create a mental framework that influences our actions and decisions. The power of the mind is well documented in psychology and spirituality. By harnessing the power of our mind, we can create the reality we desire, including financial abundance.

2. The Mindset-Wealth Connection

Our mindset has a direct impact on our wealth. A positive and prosperous mindset creates a positive and prosperous reality. A negative and scarcity mindset creates a negative and scarcity reality. Our mindset affects our financial habits, decisions, and outcomes. Therefore, developing a prosperous mindset is essential for achieving financial success and fulfillment.

3. The Prosperous Mindset

A prosperous mindset is characterized by abundance, gratitude, self-worth, mindfulness, purpose, generosity, and faith. These qualities create a positive and abundant reality. They support good financial habits and decisions, such as budgeting, saving, investing, and giving. They also attract opportunities for wealth and success.

4. Overcoming Scarcity Mindset

A scarcity mindset is characterized by fear, lack, and limitation. It creates a negative and scarce reality. It can hold us back from achieving financial success and fulfillment. To overcome a scarcity mindset, we must identify our limiting beliefs and replace them with empowering beliefs. We must also cultivate abundance and gratitude to shift our mindset towards positivity and prosperity.

5. Mindset Techniques

There are several techniques we can use to cultivate a prosperous mindset, including:

- Affirmations: Using positive affirmations to reinforce empowering beliefs.
- Visualization: Visualizing our desired reality to manifest it into existence.
- Meditation: Cultivating mindfulness to stay present and positive.
- Gratitude: Practicing gratitude to focus on abundance and positivity.
- Self-reflection: Reflecting on our thoughts and beliefs to identify limiting beliefs and replace them with empowering ones.

6. Integrating Mindset and Wealth

Integrating mindset and wealth requires intention and effort. We must cultivate a prosperous mindset while also taking action towards our financial goals. This means developing good financial habits, such as budgeting, saving, investing, and giving. It also means taking risks and pursuing opportunities that align with our purpose and values.

Identifying Your Limiting Beliefs About Money

Our beliefs about money can greatly impact our financial success and fulfillment. Some beliefs can be empowering and supportive, while others can be limiting and detrimental. In this chapter, we will explore the concept of limiting beliefs about money and how to identify and overcome them.

1. What are Limiting Beliefs About Money?

Limiting beliefs about money are beliefs that hinder our financial success and fulfillment. They can be subconscious or conscious and can create a negative and scarcity mindset. Some examples of limiting beliefs about money are:

- Money is the root of all evil.
- Money is hard to come by.
- I'm not good with money.
- Rich people are greedy and selfish.
- I don't deserve to be wealthy.

These beliefs can hold us back from achieving financial success and fulfillment, and it's important to identify and overcome them.

2. Why Identify Limiting Beliefs About Money?

Identifying limiting beliefs about money is crucial for developing a prosperous mindset and achieving financial success and fulfillment. Limiting beliefs can create a negative and scarcity mindset, which can lead to bad financial habits and decisions. By identifying and overcoming limiting beliefs, we can replace them with empowering beliefs and shift towards a positive and abundant mindset.

3. How to Identify Limiting Beliefs About Money?

Identifying limiting beliefs about money can be challenging because they can be subconscious. However, there are several techniques we can use to uncover them:

- Journaling: Writing down our thoughts and feelings about money can reveal limiting beliefs.
- Self-reflection: Reflecting on our past experiences with money can identify limiting beliefs.
- Mindfulness: Paying attention to our thoughts and emotions can reveal limiting beliefs.
- Seeking feedback: Asking trusted friends or family members for feedback on our beliefs about money can uncover limiting beliefs.

4. Overcoming Limiting Beliefs About Money

Overcoming limiting beliefs about money requires a conscious effort to replace them with empowering beliefs. Here are some steps we can take to overcome limiting beliefs:

- Acknowledge the belief: Recognize the limiting belief and how it has impacted your financial life.
- Challenge the belief: Ask yourself if the belief is true and where it comes from.
- Replace the belief: Replace the limiting belief with an empowering belief that supports your financial success and fulfillment.
- Take action: Take action towards your financial goals, despite the limiting belief.

5. Developing Empowering Beliefs About Money

Developing empowering beliefs about money is crucial for achieving financial success and fulfillment. Empowering beliefs can create a positive and abundant mindset, which can lead to good financial habits and decisions. Here are some empowering beliefs about money:

- Money is a tool for creating abundance and fulfilling my purpose.
- I am capable of managing my money wisely and making it grow.
- Wealth is a reflection of my self-worth and my ability to contribute to society.
- Rich people are generous and use their wealth for the greater good.
- I deserve to be wealthy and enjoy the abundance that life has to offer.

Identifying and overcoming limiting beliefs about money is essential for developing a prosperous mindset and achieving financial success and fulfillment. By acknowledging, challenging, and replacing limiting beliefs with empowering beliefs, we can shift towards a positive and abundant mindset that supports our financial goals.

The Power of Gratitude in Financial Abundance

The Science of Gratitude and Its Impact on the Brain

Gratitude is often described as a spiritual or philosophical concept, but it has also been studied extensively in the scientific community. Research has shown that cultivating gratitude can have a profound impact on the brain and overall well-being. In this chapter, we will explore the science of gratitude and its impact on the brain.

1. What is Gratitude?

Gratitude is the practice of acknowledging and appreciating the good in one's life. It involves recognizing the positive aspects of our experiences and expressing appreciation for them. Gratitude can be expressed through simple acts, such as saying "thank you" or writing a gratitude journal.

2. The Science of Gratitude

The study of gratitude has become a growing area of research in recent years, with numerous studies demonstrating the benefits of cultivating gratitude. Some of the findings include:

- Improved physical health: Studies have shown that practicing gratitude can improve sleep, lower

14

blood pressure, and reduce symptoms of depression and anxiety.

- Improved emotional well-being: Gratitude has been linked to increased feelings of happiness, contentment, and life satisfaction.
- Strengthened social connections: Gratitude can foster positive social connections by promoting feelings of kindness, empathy, and compassion towards others.
- Increased resilience: Gratitude can help individuals cope with stressful situations and increase their ability to bounce back from adversity.

3. The Impact of Gratitude on the Brain

The practice of gratitude has been found to have a significant impact on the brain. Specifically, studies have shown that practicing gratitude can:

- Activate the reward center of the brain: Gratitude has been found to activate the same areas of the brain associated with reward and pleasure, such as the ventral striatum and prefrontal cortex.
- Increase levels of dopamine and serotonin: These neurotransmitters are associated with feelings of pleasure, happiness, and contentment.
- Decrease activity in the amygdala: This part of the brain is associated with the stress response and negative emotions.
- Increase activity in the prefrontal cortex: This area of the brain is associated with higher-level cognitive functions, such as decision-making, problem-solving, and self-regulation.

Cultivating a Gratitude Practice for Financial Prosperity

Cultivating gratitude is a powerful practice that can improve our overall well-being, including our financial prosperity. In this chapter, we will explore how to cultivate a gratitude practice specifically for financial abundance.

1. Gratitude and Financial Prosperity

Cultivating gratitude can be an effective way to attract financial abundance into our lives. By focusing on the abundance that already exists in our lives, we can shift our mindset from scarcity to abundance. When we feel grateful for what we have, we attract more positive experiences into our lives.

2. Gratitude Practice for Financial Prosperity

Here are some strategies for cultivating a gratitude practice specifically for financial prosperity:

a. Create a Gratitude Journal

Keeping a gratitude journal is a powerful way to cultivate feelings of gratitude. Write down things that you are grateful for in your life, including financial blessings. This practice can help shift your mindset from scarcity to abundance and help you focus on the positive aspects of your financial situation.

b. Visualize Financial Abundance

Visualizing financial abundance is another powerful way to cultivate gratitude. Spend some time each day visualizing your financial goals as if they have already been achieved. Visualize yourself feeling grateful for your financial abundance and enjoying the benefits that come with it.

c. Express Gratitude for Financial Blessings

Take some time each day to express gratitude for the financial blessings in your life. This can be done through prayer, meditation, or simply by saying "thank you" for the abundance in your life.

d. Reframe Negative Financial Experiences

When negative financial experiences arise, try to reframe them in a positive light. Look for the lessons that can be learned from the experience and focus on the positive aspects of the situation. This can help shift your mindset from scarcity to abundance and cultivate feelings of gratitude.

e. Practice Generosity

Practicing generosity is another powerful way to cultivate feelings of gratitude and attract financial abundance into your life. When you give freely to others, you create positive energy that attracts more positive experiences into your life.

3. Integrating Gratitude into Your Financial Habits

In addition to cultivating a gratitude practice, it is important to integrate gratitude into your financial habits. This can include:

- Tracking your expenses and income with gratitude: Instead of focusing on the money that is leaving your bank account, focus on the abundance that is coming into your life.
- Budgeting with gratitude: Create a budget that reflects your values and priorities, and focus on the positive aspects of the budget.
- Giving with gratitude: When you give to charity or support causes that you care about, do so with a sense of gratitude for the abundance in your life.

How Gratitude Can Shift Your Financial Perspective

Gratitude is a powerful tool that can transform the way we view our financial situation, leading to a more positive and abundant outlook.

1. Gratitude and Mindset

Gratitude is an attitude of appreciation and thankfulness for the good things in our lives. When we focus on gratitude, we shift our mindset from one of scarcity to one of abundance. Instead of focusing on what we don't have, we focus on what we do have, which creates feelings of contentment and fulfillment.

2. Gratitude and Financial Perspective

Gratitude can also shift our financial perspective. When we cultivate feelings of gratitude, we become more aware of the abundance in our lives, including our financial blessings. Instead of focusing on what we lack, we appreciate the financial resources we do have, such as a steady income, a comfortable home, or supportive relationships.

3. Gratitude and Financial Goals

Gratitude can also help us achieve our financial goals. When we focus on the positive aspects of our financial situation, we are more likely to take action towards achieving our financial goals. This is because we feel more motivated and confident in our ability to create financial abundance in our lives.

4. Gratitude and Financial Habits

Gratitude can also transform our financial habits. When we cultivate gratitude, we are more likely to make financial decisions that align with our values and priorities. For example, we may choose to spend money on experiences that bring us joy rather than on material possessions that don't contribute to our happiness.

5. Gratitude and Wealth Consciousness

Gratitude can also help us develop a wealth consciousness. Wealth consciousness is the mindset that we have an abundance of financial resources available to us. This mindset attracts more abundance into our lives, creating a positive feedback loop of financial prosperity.

6. Strategies for Cultivating Gratitude

There are many strategies for cultivating gratitude, including:

a. Keeping a gratitude journal: Write down things you are grateful for each day, including your financial blessings.

b. Practicing mindfulness: Focus on the present moment and appreciate the abundance in your life.

c. Giving back: When you give to others, you create a sense of gratitude and abundance in your life.

d. Reframing negative thoughts: Look for the lessons in negative experiences and focus on the positive aspects of the situation.

e. Surrounding yourself with positivity: Spend time with people who have a positive attitude towards money and financial abundance.

Gratitude is a powerful tool that can shift our financial perspective and transform the way we view our financial situation. By cultivating feelings of gratitude, we become more aware of the abundance in our lives, which leads to a more positive and abundant outlook. Gratitude can help us achieve our financial goals, transform our financial habits, and develop a wealth consciousness. By incorporating gratitude into our daily lives, we can create a more fulfilling and prosperous financial future.

The Importance of Financial Education

Understanding the Basics of Financial Literacy

In this chapter, we will explore the basics of financial literacy. Financial literacy is the ability to understand and manage your financial resources effectively. It is an essential life skill that can help you achieve your financial goals and create a stable financial future.

1. What is Financial Literacy?

Financial literacy is the knowledge and skills required to manage your financial resources effectively. It involves understanding financial concepts such as budgeting, saving, investing, and debt management.

2. The Importance of Financial Literacy

Financial literacy is essential for creating a stable financial future. Without financial literacy, you may struggle with managing your finances, making it difficult to achieve your financial goals. Financial literacy can also help you avoid financial mistakes that can lead to debt and financial hardship.

3. Financial Literacy and Mindset

Financial literacy is closely linked to mindset. Your mindset towards money can impact your financial literacy. For example, if you believe that you are not good with money, you may be less likely to seek out financial education and take steps to improve your financial literacy.

4. Financial Literacy and Financial Goals

Financial literacy can help you achieve your financial goals. When you have a strong understanding of financial concepts, you can create a budget, save for the future, and invest wisely. This can help you achieve financial milestones such as purchasing a home, starting a business, or saving for retirement.

5. Basic Financial Concepts

Some of the basic financial concepts that are important for financial literacy include:

a. Budgeting: creating a plan for your income and expenses

b. Saving: setting aside money for the future

c. Investing: putting your money to work to create wealth

d. Debt management: managing your debt to avoid financial hardship

e. Credit management: maintaining good credit to access financial resources

6. Strategies for Improving Financial Literacy

There are many strategies for improving your financial literacy, including:

a. Reading financial books and articles

b. Attending financial workshops and seminars

c. Working with a financial advisor or planner

d. Taking online courses or classes

e. Practicing good financial habits, such as budgeting and saving

Financial literacy is an essential life skill that can help you achieve your financial goals and create a stable financial future. By understanding basic financial concepts and implementing good financial habits, you can improve your financial literacy and take control of your financial resources. Financial literacy is not only about money, but also about mindset and personal growth. By incorporating financial literacy into your daily life, you can create a more fulfilling and prosperous financial future.

The Link Between Financial Education and Wealth Creation

Wealth creation is the process of building and accumulating assets over time. Financial education is the knowledge and skills required to manage your financial resources effectively. When combined, financial education and wealth creation can help you achieve financial success and create a stable financial future.

1. What is Financial Education?

Financial education is the knowledge and skills required to manage your financial resources effectively. It involves understanding financial concepts such as budgeting, saving, investing, and debt management.

2. The Importance of Financial Education

Financial education is essential for creating a stable financial future. Without financial education, you may struggle with managing your finances, making it difficult to achieve your financial goals. Financial education can also help you avoid financial mistakes that can lead to debt and financial hardship.

3. Financial Education and Wealth Creation

Financial education is closely linked to wealth creation. When you have a strong understanding of financial concepts, you can make informed decisions about your finances. This can help you create a solid financial foundation and build wealth over time.

4. Benefits of Financial Education for Wealth Creation

There are many benefits of financial education for wealth creation, including:

a. Understanding financial concepts: Financial education can help you understand financial concepts such as budgeting, saving, investing, and debt management. This knowledge can help you make informed decisions about your finances and create a solid financial foundation.

b. Making informed financial decisions: When you have a strong understanding of financial concepts, you can make informed decisions about your finances. This can help you avoid financial mistakes and create wealth over time.

c. Creating a financial plan: Financial education can help you create a financial plan that is tailored to your financial goals and needs. This can help you achieve your financial goals and build wealth over time.

d. Accessing financial resources: Financial education can help you access financial resources such as loans, credit, and investment opportunities. This can help you build wealth over time and achieve your financial goals.

Financial education is essential for creating a stable financial future and building wealth over time. By understanding basic financial concepts and implementing good financial habits, you can improve your financial education and take control of your financial resources. Financial education is not only about money, but also about mindset and personal growth. By incorporating financial education into your daily life, you can create a more fulfilling and prosperous financial future.

Strategies for Building Your Financial Knowledge

In this chapter, we will discuss the strategies for building your financial knowledge. Financial knowledge is essential for managing your money effectively and building wealth over time. By improving your financial knowledge, you can make informed decisions about your finances and create a stable financial future. Here are some strategies for building your financial knowledge:

1. Read Financial Books and Articles

One of the best ways to improve your financial knowledge is by reading financial books and articles. There are countless books and articles available that cover a range of financial topics, from basic personal finance to more advanced investing strategies. Reading financial books and articles can help you learn new concepts and gain insights into financial planning and wealth creation.

2. Attend Financial Workshops and Seminars

Attending financial workshops and seminars can also help you build your financial knowledge. These events are designed to provide you with practical tips and strategies for managing your finances and building wealth. You can also network with other like-minded individuals who are interested in financial planning and wealth creation.

3. Work with a Financial Advisor or Planner

Working with a financial advisor or planner can also help you build your financial knowledge. A financial advisor can provide you with personalized advice and guidance on managing your finances and building wealth. They can also help you create a financial plan that is tailored to your financial goals and needs.

4. Take Online Courses or Classes

Online courses and classes can also help you improve your financial knowledge. Many universities and financial institutions offer online courses and classes that cover a range of financial topics. These courses can help you learn new concepts and gain practical skills for managing your finances and building wealth.

5. Practice Good Financial Habits

Practicing good financial habits can also help you build your financial knowledge. By developing good habits, such as budgeting, saving, and investing, you can gain a better understanding of how money works and how to manage it effectively. You can also learn from your own experiences and mistakes, which can help you improve your financial knowledge over time.

6. Cultivate a Growth Mindset

Finally, cultivating a growth mindset is essential for building your financial knowledge. A growth mindset is the belief that your abilities and skills can be developed through dedication and hard work. By cultivating a growth mindset, you can approach financial learning with a positive and open attitude, which can help you learn and grow over time.

Building your financial knowledge is essential for managing your finances effectively and building wealth over time. By reading financial books and articles, attending financial workshops and seminars, working with a financial advisor or planner, taking online courses or classes, practicing good financial habits, and cultivating a growth mindset, you can improve your financial knowledge and achieve your financial goals. Remember, financial education is not only about money, but also about mindset and personal growth. By incorporating financial education into your daily life, you can create a more fulfilling and prosperous financial future.

The Role of Mindfulness in Financial Success

Mindfulness and Its Connection to Financial Well-being

In recent years, mindfulness has become a popular practice for improving mental health and reducing stress. However, mindfulness can also have a significant impact on your financial well-being. In this chapter, we will explore the connection between mindfulness and financial well-being and how you can incorporate mindfulness into your financial life.

What is Mindfulness?

Mindfulness is the practice of being present and fully engaged in the current moment. It involves paying attention to your thoughts, emotions, and sensations without judgment or distraction. Mindfulness can help you develop greater self-awareness and emotional regulation, which can lead to improved mental and physical health.

The Connection Between Mindfulness and Financial Well-being

Financial well-being is the state of being in control of your finances and having the resources to achieve your financial goals. Mindfulness can have a significant impact on your financial well-being in the following ways:

1. Reduce Impulsive Spending

Mindfulness can help you become more aware of your spending habits and reduce impulsive spending. When you are mindful of your thoughts and emotions, you can recognize when you are experiencing a desire to spend money and pause to consider whether it aligns with your financial goals.

2. Increase Savings

Mindfulness can also help you increase your savings. By being present in the moment, you can focus on your financial goals and develop a greater appreciation for the value of saving. You can also develop a better understanding of your spending habits and identify areas where you can cut back to increase your savings.

3. Improve Financial Decision-making

Mindfulness can help you make better financial decisions by reducing the impact of biases and emotions. When you are mindful, you are better able to consider all the factors involved in a financial decision and make a decision based on your long-term goals rather than short-term emotions.

4. Reduce Financial Stress

Mindfulness can also reduce financial stress by helping you manage your emotions and develop a greater sense of control over your finances. By being present in the moment, you can reduce anxiety about the future and develop a greater sense of peace and contentment.

Incorporating Mindfulness into Your Financial Life

Here are some ways you can incorporate mindfulness into your financial life:

1. Practice Mindful Spending

Before making a purchase, take a moment to consider whether it aligns with your financial goals and values. Ask yourself if it is a need or a want and whether it is worth the cost.

2. Practice Gratitude

Gratitude is a key component of mindfulness and can help you develop a greater appreciation for the resources you have. Take time each day to express gratitude for the financial resources you have, whether it is a roof over your head, food on the table, or the ability to save for your future.

3. Practice Mindful Budgeting

When creating a budget, be mindful of your financial goals and values. Consider how your budget aligns with your long-term goals and how it can help you achieve financial well-being.

4. Practice Mindful Investing

When investing, be mindful of your risk tolerance and your long-term goals. Consider how each investment aligns with your values and whether it is a good fit for your portfolio.

Mindfulness can have a significant impact on your financial well-being by reducing impulsive spending, increasing savings, improving financial decision-making, and reducing financial stress. By incorporating mindfulness into your financial life, you can develop greater awareness and control over your finances and achieve greater financial well-being. Remember, mindfulness is not only about your finances, but also about your overall well-being and personal growth. By cultivating mindfulness, you can create a more fulfilling and prosperous life.

How to Incorporate Mindfulness into Your Money Habits

In today's fast-paced world, it's easy to get caught up in the hustle and bustle of everyday life. Many of us live on autopilot, going through the motions without much thought or intentionality. This can be especially true when it comes to our finances. We spend money without really thinking about where it's going, and before we know it, we're left wondering where all our money went.

But there's a solution to this mindless spending, and it's called mindfulness. Mindfulness is the practice of being present and fully engaged in the moment. It's about paying attention to what's happening right now, without judgment or distraction. And when it comes to our money habits, mindfulness can be a powerful tool for improving our financial well-being.

In this chapter, we'll explore how you can incorporate mindfulness into your money habits, so you can develop a more intentional and mindful relationship with your finances.

The Importance of Mindful Money Habits

Before we dive into specific strategies for incorporating mindfulness into your money habits, let's first explore why this practice is so important. Mindful money habits can help you:

1. Increase awareness: Mindfulness helps you become more aware of your thoughts, feelings, and actions. When you're mindful of your spending habits, you'll be better equipped to notice patterns and behaviors that may be contributing to financial stress.
2. Make better financial decisions: Mindful money habits help you make more informed financial decisions. By taking the time to assess your options and consider the potential consequences of your choices, you can make decisions that align with your long-term financial goals.
3. Reduce stress: Financial stress is a common problem for many people, and it can have a significant impact on overall well-being. Mindful money habits can help you manage stress by reducing impulsive spending and promoting a greater sense of financial control.

Strategies for Incorporating Mindfulness into Your Money Habits

Now that we've established the importance of mindful money habits, let's explore some specific strategies for incorporating this practice into your financial routine.

1. Practice Gratitude: Gratitude is a powerful mindfulness practice that can help you develop a more positive relationship with your finances. Take time each day to reflect on what you're grateful for financially, whether it's a steady income, a supportive partner, or a comfortable home.

2. Track Your Spending: Mindful money habits require awareness, and one way to develop this awareness is by tracking your spending. Keep a journal or use a budgeting app to track where your money is going, so you can identify patterns and areas where you may need to adjust your spending habits.

3. Set Intentions: Mindful money habits involve setting intentions for how you want to spend and save your money. Take time to reflect on your financial goals and values, and set intentions that align with these priorities.

4. Engage Your Senses: Mindfulness is all about being present in the moment, and engaging your senses can help you cultivate this presence. When making financial decisions, take time to engage your senses. Notice the texture of your money, the sound of coins jingling in your pocket, or the sight of a beautiful sunset as you consider your financial options.

5. Practice Patience: Mindful money habits require patience and an understanding that financial goals take time to achieve. Practice patience by

avoiding impulsive purchases and focusing on the long-term benefits of your financial decisions.

Incorporating mindfulness into your money habits can be a powerful tool for improving your financial well-being. By developing a more intentional and mindful relationship with your finances, you can increase awareness, make better financial decisions, and reduce stress. So take some time to reflect on your current money habits, and consider

Mindful Spending: A Guide to Conscious Consumption

Money is a tool that we use to meet our needs and fulfill our desires. However, it is easy to get carried away and overspend, leading to financial stress and anxiety. Mindful spending is a practice of being fully present and aware of our spending habits, so we can make more intentional and conscious choices about how we use our money. In this chapter, we will explore the concept of mindful spending and how it can contribute to our financial well-being.

Understanding Mindful Spending:

Mindful spending involves being aware of our thoughts, emotions, and behaviors related to money. It means taking the time to reflect on our values, priorities, and goals before making any purchasing decisions. This practice helps us avoid impulsive buying and unnecessary expenses, which can add up over time and drain our financial resources.

When we practice mindful spending, we also become more aware of the impact of our spending on ourselves and others. We consider the environmental and social consequences of our purchases and choose products and services that align with our values and beliefs.

Benefits of Mindful Spending:

Mindful spending offers several benefits, both for our financial and overall well-being. Here are some of the advantages of incorporating mindfulness into our spending habits:

1. Increased awareness: When we pay attention to our spending habits, we become more aware of our financial situation and can make more informed decisions about our money.
2. Reduced stress: Mindful spending helps us avoid unnecessary expenses, which can reduce financial stress and anxiety.
3. Improved relationships: By being mindful of our spending, we can make more conscious choices that align with our values, which can improve our relationships with ourselves and others.
4. Better financial management: Mindful spending allows us to prioritize our expenses and manage our finances more effectively.

Strategies for Practicing Mindful Spending:

Here are some strategies to help you incorporate mindful spending into your daily life:

1. Set financial goals: Identify your short-term and long-term financial goals, and make sure your spending aligns with those goals.
2. Create a budget: Develop a budget that reflects your income, expenses, and financial goals. Use this budget as a guide for your spending decisions.
3. Reflect on your values: Consider your values and beliefs, and make sure your spending reflects those values.
4. Delay gratification: Before making any purchases, take a moment to reflect on whether the item is a need or a want. Consider waiting a day or two before making the purchase to avoid impulse buying.
5. Practice gratitude: When making a purchase, take a moment to express gratitude for the money you have and the ability to make the purchase.
6. Choose quality over quantity: Consider the quality and durability of a product before making a purchase. Investing in high-quality items can save money in the long run.
7. Consider the environmental and social impact: Before making a purchase, consider the environmental and social impact of the product or service. Choose products and services that align with your values and beliefs.

Mindful spending is a powerful tool for achieving financial well-being and living a more conscious and intentional life. By practicing mindfulness in our spending habits, we can increase our awareness, reduce stress, improve our relationships, and manage our finances more effectively. Incorporate these strategies into your daily life to cultivate a more mindful and prosperous relationship with money.

The Power of Visualization for Wealth Creation

Using Visualization Techniques to Attract Abundance

In the pursuit of financial abundance, many people turn to visualization techniques to help them manifest their desires. Visualization is the process of creating mental images or scenarios in your mind to achieve a specific goal. By imagining yourself in a desired financial state, you can begin to attract abundance and bring your vision to life.

Visualization is a powerful tool that can help you shift your mindset and beliefs about money. When you visualize, you are sending a clear message to the universe that you are ready and willing to receive abundance. By focusing on what you want, you are more likely to attract those things into your life.

Here are some tips on how to use visualization techniques to attract abundance:

1. Set an intention: Before you begin visualizing, it is important to set a clear intention for what you want to manifest. This could be a specific financial goal, such as earning a certain amount of money, or a more general desire, such as feeling financially secure. By setting an intention, you are providing a clear focus for your visualization practice.

2. Create a clear image: Once you have set your intention, begin to create a clear mental image of what you want. Imagine yourself in your desired financial state, whether it is having a large bank account balance or being debt-free. Focus on the details of your vision, such as the feelings, sights, and sounds associated with it.

3. Engage your senses: Visualization is most effective when you engage all of your senses. As you create your mental image, imagine what it feels like to be in your desired financial state. What do you see around you? What do you hear? What do you smell and taste? By engaging your senses, you are making your visualization more vivid and real.

4. Repeat your visualization daily: To manifest your desires, it is important to make your visualization a daily practice. Take a few minutes each day to imagine yourself in your desired financial state. This will help you to stay focused and connected to your vision.

5. Trust the process: Visualization is not an instant fix for financial problems. It is a practice that requires patience and trust. By consistently visualizing your desires, you are sending a message to the universe that you are ready to receive abundance. Trust that the universe will bring you what you need, when you need it.

Incorporating visualization techniques into your daily routine can help you to attract abundance and achieve your financial goals. By focusing on what you want, engaging your senses, and trusting the process, you can create a powerful manifestation practice that will bring you financial prosperity.

Visualization as a Tool for Creating Your Ideal Financial Future

Visualizing your ideal financial future can be a powerful tool in achieving your financial goals. It involves creating a mental image of the future you desire and focusing your thoughts and emotions on that image. This technique helps you to align your thoughts, beliefs, and actions with the reality you want to create. In this chapter, we will explore the benefits of visualization and how to use it to create your ideal financial future.

Benefits of Visualization Visualization has been used for centuries as a tool for manifestation and creating the reality we desire. It has been used in sports psychology to help athletes visualize their success, in business to help entrepreneurs visualize their success, and in personal development to help individuals create the life they want. When it comes to financial success, visualization can be a powerful tool for the following reasons:

1. Clarifies your goals: Visualization helps you to clarify what you want to achieve financially. By creating a mental image of your ideal financial future, you can focus on the specific outcomes you want to achieve.
2. Helps you to stay motivated: Visualizing your ideal financial future helps to keep you motivated to achieve your goals. When you can see the end result in your mind, it makes it easier to keep moving towards that goal.

3. Attracts abundance: Visualization helps you to align your thoughts and emotions with abundance. By focusing on the abundance you desire, you can attract it into your life.
4. Helps you to overcome limiting beliefs: Visualization can help you to overcome limiting beliefs about money and wealth. By creating a mental image of the reality you desire, you can replace negative beliefs with positive ones.

How to Use Visualization to Create Your Ideal Financial Future:

Using visualization to create your ideal financial future involves the following steps:

1. Clarify your financial goals: The first step is to clarify your financial goals. Write down specific goals you want to achieve, such as owning a home, starting a business, or retiring comfortably. Make sure these goals are specific, measurable, and achievable.
2. Create a mental image: Once you have clarified your goals, create a mental image of what your ideal financial future looks like. Imagine yourself achieving these goals and experiencing the emotions that come with that success.
3. Engage your senses: Engage all your senses in your visualization. Imagine what it would look like, feel like, smell like, and sound like to achieve your financial goals. The more you can engage your senses, the more real your visualization will feel.
4. Focus on the positive: Focus on the positive outcomes you want to achieve rather than the

negative ones you want to avoid. This helps you to attract abundance into your life and overcome limiting beliefs.

5. Practice regularly: Visualization is a skill that requires practice. Set aside time each day to visualize your ideal financial future. The more you practice, the more effective your visualization will be.

6. Take inspired action: Visualization is not a substitute for action. Take inspired action towards your financial goals. Use your visualization to inspire and motivate you to take action towards your goals.

Visualization can be a powerful tool in creating your ideal financial future. By clarifying your goals, creating a mental image, engaging your senses, focusing on the positive, practicing regularly, and taking inspired action, you can attract abundance into your life and overcome limiting beliefs about money and wealth.

How to Manifest Wealth Through Visualization

Visualization is a powerful tool that can help you manifest wealth and abundance. It involves creating a mental image of your desired outcome and holding it in your mind until it becomes a reality. The idea behind visualization is that your thoughts and beliefs shape your reality, and by focusing on positive outcomes, you can attract them into your life.

In this chapter, we will explore the basics of visualization and how you can use it to manifest wealth. We will also look at some practical techniques you can use to enhance your visualization practice and achieve your financial goals.

Understanding the Basics of Visualization

Visualization is a technique that has been used for centuries to achieve various goals, from physical healing to spiritual enlightenment. It involves using your imagination to create a mental image of your desired outcome. When you visualize, you are essentially programming your subconscious mind with positive thoughts and beliefs that support your goals.

Visualization works on the principle that your thoughts and emotions create an energy field that attracts similar experiences into your life. By focusing on positive thoughts and feelings, you can create a positive energy field that attracts abundance and prosperity.

To get started with visualization, you need to first identify your goals and desires. This could be anything from financial abundance to a specific career or relationship goal. Once you have identified your goal, you can create a mental image of what it would look and feel like to achieve it.

Practical Techniques for Enhancing Your Visualization Practice

Here are some practical techniques you can use to enhance your visualization practice and manifest wealth:

1. Create a vision board: A vision board is a visual representation of your goals and desires. It can include images, quotes, and affirmations that inspire and motivate you. By looking at your vision board every day, you can reinforce your positive thoughts and beliefs and attract the experiences you desire.

2. Use affirmations: Affirmations are positive statements that reinforce your desired outcome. For example, you could say, "I am worthy of financial abundance" or "I attract wealth and prosperity into my life." By repeating these affirmations daily, you can reprogram your subconscious mind with positive thoughts and beliefs.

3. Practice gratitude: Gratitude is a powerful emotion that can help you attract abundance into your life. By focusing on what you are grateful for, you create a positive energy field that attracts more positive experiences. You can practice gratitude by writing in a gratitude journal, thanking the universe for your blessings, or simply taking a moment to appreciate the good things in your life.

4. Use guided visualizations: Guided visualizations are pre-recorded audio programs that take you on a journey of self-discovery and transformation. They can help you release negative beliefs and emotions that are blocking your abundance and prosperity. You can find guided visualizations online or through a coach or therapist.

Visualization is a powerful tool that can help you manifest wealth and abundance. By creating a mental image of your desired outcome and holding it in your mind, you can attract positive experiences into your life. To enhance your visualization practice, you can use techniques like creating a vision board, using affirmations, practicing gratitude, and using guided visualizations. With consistent practice and a positive mindset, you can manifest the wealth and abundance you desire.

The Abundance Mindset: Attracting Wealth and Prosperity

Understanding the Abundance Mindset

When it comes to financial abundance, it's easy to get caught up in a scarcity mindset that tells us there's never enough to go around. But what if we shift our thinking to one of abundance? What if we believe that there is always enough to go around and that we can attract and create more wealth? This is the foundation of the abundance mindset, which is about shifting our beliefs and perceptions about money and the world around us. In this chapter, we will explore the abundance mindset in more detail and provide strategies for cultivating this way of thinking.

Understanding the Abundance Mindset:

The abundance mindset is about believing that there is more than enough to go around, that there are endless possibilities and opportunities for financial success, and that wealth and prosperity are available to everyone who is willing to seek it out. It's the opposite of the scarcity mindset, which is based on fear, lack, and limitation.

To cultivate the abundance mindset, we must first recognize that our thoughts and beliefs about money can impact our ability to attract and create wealth. If we believe that money is scarce, that there is never enough, or that we don't deserve financial abundance, then we are likely to struggle with our finances. On the other hand, if we believe that money is abundant, that there are always opportunities to create wealth, and that we deserve financial success, then we are more likely to attract abundance into our lives.

Strategies for Cultivating the Abundance Mindset:

1. Gratitude: Cultivating gratitude is a powerful way to shift our mindset from scarcity to abundance. When we focus on what we have rather than what we lack, we begin to see the abundance that already exists in our lives. We can practice gratitude by keeping a daily gratitude journal, expressing thanks for the abundance we have, and focusing on the positive aspects of our financial situation.
2. Visualization: Visualization is a powerful tool for manifesting abundance. By visualizing our ideal financial future, we can create a mental image of what we want to attract into our lives. This can help us to focus our thoughts and actions on the things that will bring us closer to our financial goals.
3. Affirmations: Affirmations are positive statements that we repeat to ourselves to reinforce a positive mindset. By using affirmations related to abundance and prosperity, we can reprogram our minds to believe that we are deserving of financial success and that there is always enough to go around.
4. Abundance Mentality: Adopting an abundance mentality means believing that there is always enough to go around and that success and wealth are not limited resources. By embracing this mindset, we can let go of fears and limiting

beliefs that may be holding us back from achieving our financial goals.

The abundance mindset is about shifting our beliefs and perceptions about money and the world around us. By recognizing the abundance that already exists in our lives, cultivating gratitude, using visualization techniques, and adopting an abundance mentality, we can attract and create more wealth and prosperity. Remember, financial abundance is available to everyone who is willing to seek it out.

How to Shift Your Mindset from Scarcity to Abundance

The mindset of scarcity is one that is deeply ingrained in many of us, and it can be difficult to shake off. This mentality is characterized by fear, anxiety, and a belief that there is never enough of anything, including money. The good news is that it is possible to shift your mindset from scarcity to abundance, and with some effort and practice, you can create a more positive and prosperous relationship with money. In this chapter, we will explore some techniques that you can use to help make this shift.

1. Recognize your scarcity mindset

The first step in shifting your mindset from scarcity to abundance is to become aware of your current thought patterns. Do you often worry about money, even if you have enough? Do you feel a sense of fear or anxiety when you think about your financial future? Do you find yourself obsessing over small expenses, or feeling like you can never have enough? These are all signs of a scarcity mindset.

2. Reframe your thoughts

Once you have identified your scarcity mindset, the next step is to start reframing your thoughts. Instead of focusing on what you lack, focus on what you have. This means acknowledging the good things in your life, such as your health, your relationships, and your talents. Recognize that you have already achieved many things, and that you are capable of achieving more.

3. Practice gratitude

Gratitude is a powerful tool for shifting your mindset from scarcity to abundance. By focusing on the things you are grateful for, you can start to see the abundance in your life. Take a few moments each day to reflect on the things you are thankful for, and try to cultivate an attitude of gratitude in your daily life.

4. Visualize abundance

Visualization is another powerful tool for shifting your mindset from scarcity to abundance. Spend some time each day visualizing the abundance you want in your life. See yourself surrounded by wealth, success, and prosperity. Imagine yourself achieving your financial goals, and feel the joy and happiness that comes with it.

5.   Take action

Shifting your mindset from scarcity to abundance requires more than just changing your thoughts. You also need to take action. This means setting clear financial goals, creating a plan to achieve them, and taking steps each day to move closer to your goals. When you take action towards your goals, you reinforce the belief that you are capable of achieving abundance.

6.   Surround yourself with abundance

Finally, surround yourself with abundance. This means surrounding yourself with people who have a positive mindset about money, and who can offer support and encouragement as you work towards your financial goals. It also means surrounding yourself with symbols of abundance, such as images of wealth and prosperity, and creating an environment that reflects your desire for abundance.

Shifting your mindset from scarcity to abundance is a process that requires effort and practice. By recognizing your scarcity mindset, reframing your thoughts, practicing gratitude, visualizing abundance, taking action, and surrounding yourself with abundance, you can create a more positive and prosperous relationship with money. Remember that abundance is not just about money, but about a mindset that recognizes the abundance in all areas of life.

The Benefits of Living in an Abundant State of Mind

In the pursuit of financial abundance, it is essential to cultivate an abundant state of mind. By shifting our perspective from scarcity to abundance, we open ourselves up to a world of possibilities and opportunities. Living in an abundant state of mind has numerous benefits, not just for our financial well-being but for our overall happiness and well-being.

One of the primary benefits of living in an abundant state of mind is increased positivity and optimism. When we focus on abundance, we begin to see the world as a place of limitless opportunities and possibilities. This mindset helps us to overcome negative thoughts and self-doubt, leading to greater confidence and self-assurance.

Another benefit of living in an abundant state of mind is a greater sense of gratitude. When we focus on abundance, we become more aware of the abundance that already exists in our lives, leading to a greater sense of appreciation for what we have. This, in turn, helps us to attract more abundance into our lives.

Living in an abundant state of mind also helps us to become more creative and resourceful. When we see the world as a place of endless possibilities, we become more open-minded and willing to explore new ideas and ways of thinking. This mindset helps us to find innovative solutions to challenges and overcome obstacles on our path to financial abundance.

In addition to these benefits, living in an abundant state of mind also helps us to attract abundance into our lives. As we focus on abundance and visualize our ideal financial future, we begin to attract the people, resources, and opportunities necessary to make that vision a reality. This is because our thoughts and beliefs create a vibrational energy that attracts similar energies into our lives.

Finally, living in an abundant state of mind helps us to live a more fulfilling and purposeful life. When we are focused on abundance, we are more likely to pursue our passions and live a life that is true to our values and beliefs. This leads to greater satisfaction and fulfillment, both in our personal and financial lives.

Living in an abundant state of mind is essential for achieving financial abundance and overall well-being. By focusing on abundance, we can increase positivity and optimism, cultivate a greater sense of gratitude, become more creative and resourceful, attract abundance into our lives, and live a more fulfilling and purposeful life.

Building a Solid Financial Foundation

The Importance of Building Financial Reserves

Financial reserves are an essential aspect of financial well-being. Having a financial reserve provides a sense of security and peace of mind that can help you weather financial storms and unexpected expenses. In this chapter, we will explore why building financial reserves is so important, and how to go about doing so.

The Need for Financial Reserves

The truth is, life is unpredictable. Emergencies can happen at any time, whether it's an unexpected medical expense, a car repair, or a job loss. Without adequate financial reserves, these events can be a major setback that can put you in debt or cause financial stress.

Moreover, building financial reserves can also give you the freedom to pursue opportunities, such as starting a business or investing in a new venture. Without a reserve, you may be limited in your ability to take risks or make long-term plans.

The Benefits of Building Financial Reserves

Building a financial reserve has many benefits. It helps you prepare for emergencies, and it also helps you achieve your long-term financial goals. Here are some of the key benefits of building financial reserves:

1. Peace of mind: Knowing that you have a financial cushion can provide a sense of security and reduce financial stress.
2. Flexibility: With a reserve, you have the flexibility to make important financial decisions without the fear of running out of money.
3. Protection against unexpected expenses: A financial reserve can help you cover unexpected expenses without going into debt or using credit cards with high-interest rates.
4. Ability to take advantage of opportunities: With a reserve, you may have the resources to take advantage of unexpected opportunities or to invest in your future.

Building financial reserves is an essential aspect of financial well-being. It provides a sense of security, flexibility, and the ability to pursue opportunities. By setting a goal, creating a budget, automating your savings, considering high-yield savings accounts, and avoiding dipping into your reserve, you can build a solid financial foundation that will help you achieve your long-term financial goals.

Strategies for Creating a Budget and Sticking to It

Creating and sticking to a budget is an important step towards financial stability and abundance. A budget allows you to control your spending, save money for future goals, and avoid debt. However, it can be challenging to create a budget that works for you and stick to it over time. In this chapter, we will discuss some strategies for creating a budget and sticking to it in a mindful and spiritual way.

1. Set Your Financial Goals

The first step in creating a budget is to set your financial goals. What do you want to achieve with your money? Do you want to pay off debt, save for a down payment on a house, or build an emergency fund? Once you have a clear idea of your financial goals, you can create a budget that supports them.

2. Track Your Expenses

To create an effective budget, you need to have a clear understanding of your current spending habits. Start by tracking your expenses for a month or two. Use a notebook or an app to record everything you spend money on, including small purchases like coffee or snacks. This will help you identify areas where you can cut back and save money.

3. Determine Your Income

To create a budget, you need to know how much money you have coming in each month. If you have a steady salary, this is easy to determine. However, if your income varies from month to month, you will need to estimate your average monthly income based on your past earnings.

4. Categorize Your Expenses

Once you have tracked your expenses and determined your income, you can start categorizing your expenses.

Common categories include housing, transportation, food, entertainment, and debt repayment. Be sure to include all of your expenses, no matter how small they may seem.

5. Set Spending Limits

Based on your income and expenses, set spending limits for each category. Be realistic and make sure you can stick to these limits. If you find that you are consistently overspending in a particular category, you may need to reevaluate your budget and adjust your spending limits accordingly.

6. Review Your Budget Regularly

A budget is not a set-it-and-forget-it tool. You should review your budget regularly and make adjustments as needed. For example, if you get a raise or start a new job, you may need to adjust your income and spending limits. Or, if you have an unexpected expense, like a car repair or medical bill, you may need to adjust your budget to accommodate it.

7. Practice Mindful Spending

Creating and sticking to a budget is not just about numbers and limits. It is also about practicing mindful spending. This means being intentional about your spending and making conscious choices about where your money goes. Before making a purchase, ask yourself if it aligns with your values and supports your financial goals. This will help you stay on track with your budget and avoid impulse purchases.

8. Use Positive Affirmations

Finally, use positive affirmations to support your budgeting efforts. Affirmations are positive statements that you repeat to yourself to shift your mindset and beliefs. For example, you might say, "I am a master of my money, and I create abundance in my life." Repeat these affirmations daily to reinforce your commitment to your budget and financial goals.

Creating a budget and sticking to it requires discipline, patience, and mindfulness. By setting clear financial goals, tracking your expenses, categorizing your spending, setting spending limits, reviewing your budget regularly, practicing mindful spending, and using positive affirmations, you can create a budget that supports your financial well-being and abundance.

Tips for Managing Debt and Building Credit

Debt is a burden that can weigh down on anyone, but it doesn't have to be a life sentence. With the right strategies and mindset, you can manage your debt and build your credit for a prosperous financial future. In this chapter, we will explore some tips for managing your debt and building your credit, while also incorporating spiritual practices to help you stay centered and grounded in your financial journey.

1. Face your debt head-on

The first step towards managing your debt is to face it head-on. Avoidance only prolongs the problem, and it can lead to increased stress and anxiety. Take a deep breath and assess your debts, including the total amount owed, interest rates, and minimum payments. It may be helpful to create a spreadsheet or use a budgeting app to keep track of your debts and payments. Approach your debt with a positive attitude, and remind yourself that you are taking steps towards financial freedom.

2. Create a repayment plan

Once you have a clear understanding of your debts, create a repayment plan. This plan should include a timeline for paying off your debts, as well as strategies for managing your cash flow. Prioritize your debts based on interest rates and focus on paying off high-interest debts first. Consider debt consolidation or balance transfers to simplify your debt and reduce interest rates. Remember to be realistic with your plan and adjust it as needed.

3. Practice self-discipline

Managing debt requires self-discipline and restraint. Avoid overspending and impulse purchases, and make a conscious effort to stay within your budget. Consider setting up automatic payments for your debts to avoid missing payments or accruing late fees. Remember, every dollar you save can be put towards paying off your debts or building your credit.

4. Monitor your credit score

Your credit score is a reflection of your creditworthiness and can affect your ability to secure loans or credit in the future. Regularly monitor your credit score and check for any errors or inaccuracies. You can request a free credit report from the three major credit bureaus once a year. Improving your credit score takes time, but consistently paying off your debts and avoiding late payments can help.

5. Utilize credit responsibly

Credit can be a powerful tool when used responsibly. However, it can also be a double-edged sword that leads to further debt and financial stress. Use credit responsibly by only charging what you can afford to pay off in full each month. Avoid opening too many credit accounts at once and resist the temptation to overspend. Remember, credit should be used to enhance your financial well-being, not to detract from it.

6. Practice gratitude and self-compassion

Managing debt and building credit can be a challenging and stressful process. It's important to practice gratitude and self-compassion along the way. Take time to reflect on your progress and acknowledge your achievements, no matter how small. Be kind to yourself and avoid self-judgment. Remember, your financial situation does not define your worth as a person.

Managing debt and building credit requires both practical strategies and a spiritual mindset. By facing your debt head-on, creating a repayment plan, practicing self-discipline, monitoring your credit score, utilizing credit responsibly, and practicing gratitude and self-compassion, you can achieve financial freedom and peace of mind. Remember, the journey towards financial well-being is a marathon, not a sprint. Stay focused, stay motivated, and trust in the process.

Cultivating a Positive Relationship with Money

The Connection Between Self-Worth and Money

Money is more than just a means of exchange; it is also a symbol of our self-worth. Our beliefs about our value and what we deserve in life can shape our financial behaviors and impact our overall financial well-being. In this chapter, we will explore the link between self-worth and money, and how improving our self-worth can lead to greater financial abundance.

The Importance of Self-Worth

Self-worth is defined as the value we place on ourselves as individuals. It is our sense of self-esteem and confidence in our abilities, strengths, and worthiness. Our level of self-worth can influence many aspects of our lives, including our relationships, career, and financial decisions.

Having a healthy level of self-worth can lead to greater financial success. When we believe in ourselves and our abilities, we are more likely to take risks, pursue opportunities, and ask for what we are worth. On the other hand, if we have low self-worth, we may settle for less than we deserve or avoid taking risks that could lead to financial growth.

The Link Between Self-Worth and Money

Our beliefs about our self-worth can have a significant impact on our financial behaviors. If we believe we are not worthy of financial success or abundance, we may engage in self-sabotaging behaviors such as overspending, avoiding financial opportunities, or settling for less than we deserve. We may also struggle to negotiate for higher pay or to ask for what we are worth in our business ventures.

Conversely, when we have a healthy level of self-worth, we are more likely to make sound financial decisions that lead to greater prosperity. We are more likely to set financial goals, create a budget, and stick to it. We are also more likely to seek out financial education and resources to help us improve our financial situation.

Improving Your Self-Worth for Greater Financial Abundance

Improving your self-worth can lead to greater financial abundance. Here are some strategies you can use to enhance your self-worth:

1. Practice self-compassion: Treat yourself with kindness and compassion. Recognize that you are not perfect and that it is okay to make mistakes. Instead of criticizing yourself for financial missteps, use them as learning opportunities to improve your financial behaviors.
2. Build your self-confidence: Take actions that help build your confidence in yourself and your abilities. Set small financial goals and work

towards achieving them. Celebrate your financial successes, no matter how small they may seem.

3. Surround yourself with positivity: Surround yourself with positive people who believe in you and your abilities. Avoid people who are negative or critical of your financial goals and aspirations.

4. Challenge your limiting beliefs: Identify any limiting beliefs you may have about your self-worth and financial success. Challenge these beliefs by questioning their validity and replacing them with positive affirmations.

5. Invest in yourself: Invest in your personal and financial growth by taking courses, attending workshops, or hiring a financial coach. This can help you improve your financial literacy and build your confidence in managing your money.

By improving your self-worth, you can shift your mindset towards greater financial abundance. Remember, you are worthy of financial success and prosperity. Believe in yourself and your abilities, and take actions that align with your financial goals and values.

How to Build a Positive Relationship with Money

Money is often viewed as a taboo topic, causing stress and anxiety for many people. However, it doesn't have to be this way. With the right mindset and approach, you can build a positive relationship with money that will benefit you in all areas of your life.

1. Embrace abundance: One of the first steps in building a positive relationship with money is to

embrace abundance. Shift your mindset from scarcity to abundance and believe that there is enough money and resources for everyone. Recognize the abundance around you and be grateful for it. This will open up opportunities for financial success.

2. Identify your money story: Your money story is the narrative you tell yourself about money, and it shapes your relationship with it. Take some time to reflect on your beliefs about money and how they were formed. Identify any limiting beliefs and work to change them.

3. Practice self-compassion: Be gentle with yourself as you work on building a positive relationship with money. Don't beat yourself up for past mistakes or financial struggles. Instead, approach yourself with kindness and compassion.

4. Set clear financial goals: Having clear financial goals can help you feel more in control of your money. Identify what you want to achieve and create a plan to get there. Break down your goals into smaller, manageable steps and celebrate your progress along the way.

5. Be mindful of your spending: Mindful spending involves being intentional and conscious about your spending habits. Before making a purchase, ask yourself if it aligns with your values and goals. Avoid impulsive buying and instead take time to consider your options.

6. Create a budget: A budget is a tool for managing your money and can help you feel more in control of your finances. Create a budget that works for your lifestyle and stick to it. Regularly review your budget and adjust it as needed.

7. Invest in yourself: Investing in yourself is an important aspect of building a positive relationship with money. Take classes, attend workshops, or hire a financial coach to improve your financial literacy and skills.
8. Practice gratitude: Gratitude can help shift your mindset from lack to abundance. Regularly practice gratitude for the money and resources you have, as well as for the opportunities to create more wealth and abundance in your life.
9. Let go of financial shame: Many people carry shame and guilt around their finances. Recognize that financial struggles are common and don't define your worth. Let go of shame and focus on creating a positive relationship with money.

By following these steps, you can build a positive relationship with money and improve your overall financial well-being. Remember to approach yourself with kindness and compassion as you work towards your financial goals.

The Benefits of a Positive Money Mindset

A positive money mindset can have a profound impact on your financial well-being and overall quality of life. When you cultivate a healthy relationship with money, you feel more in control of your financial situation, experience less stress and anxiety, and are better able to make decisions that align with your values and goals.

One of the key benefits of a positive money mindset is increased financial abundance. When you approach money with a mindset of abundance, you believe that there is always enough to go around, and that you have the power to create the financial outcomes you desire. This can lead to increased opportunities for wealth creation, as you are more likely to take risks and pursue new ventures that can help you achieve your financial goals.

Another benefit of a positive money mindset is increased gratitude and contentment. When you view money as a positive force in your life, rather than a source of stress or anxiety, you are more likely to feel grateful for the resources you have and to appreciate the blessings in your life. This can lead to a greater sense of overall well-being, as you learn to focus on the abundance and positivity in your life rather than dwelling on scarcity or lack.

A positive money mindset can also help you develop greater financial confidence and competence. When you believe that you are capable of creating wealth and managing your finances effectively, you are more likely to take steps to improve your financial situation, such as investing in your education or seeking out the advice of financial professionals. This can help you develop greater financial literacy and make more informed decisions about your money.

Ultimately, cultivating a positive money mindset is about developing a sense of abundance and gratitude, and recognizing that money is simply a tool that can help you create the life you desire. When you approach money with a positive attitude and a sense of purpose, you are more likely to experience financial abundance, well-being, and overall satisfaction with your life.

The Role of Intention in Wealth Creation

Setting Financial Goals with Intention

Setting financial goals is an essential step towards achieving financial success. Goals give us a clear direction and purpose, motivating us to take action and make progress. However, simply setting a goal is not enough. To truly achieve our financial dreams, we must set goals with intention and purpose, aligning them with our values and life vision. In this chapter, we will explore the importance of setting financial goals with intention, and provide practical guidance on how to set goals that align with your values and vision.

The Power of Intention

Intention is the driving force behind all of our actions and behaviors. It is the conscious decision to direct our energy and efforts towards a particular goal or outcome. When we set goals with intention, we are declaring our commitment to achieving something that is aligned with our values and life vision. Intention sets the tone for our financial goals, ensuring that they are meaningful, purposeful, and aligned with our highest aspirations.

When we set goals with intention, we also set in motion a powerful manifestation process. The energy and focus we direct towards our goals attract more of what we want into our lives. As we focus our attention on achieving our financial goals, we become more aware of opportunities and possibilities that can help us get there. This is the power of intention in action.

Aligning Your Goals with Your Values

To set financial goals with intention, it's important to start by clarifying your values. Your values are the principles and beliefs that guide your life and shape your priorities. When you align your financial goals with your values, you create a powerful synergy that helps you stay motivated and committed to your goals.

Start by asking yourself what is most important to you in life. What are your core values? What brings you joy and fulfillment? Then, consider how your financial goals can support these values. For example, if you value freedom and independence, you may set a financial goal of creating a passive income stream that allows you to work less and enjoy more leisure time.

Crafting a Vision for Your Financial Future

Another essential step in setting financial goals with intention is to create a vision for your financial future. A vision is a vivid, compelling image of what you want to create in your life. It is a detailed description of the future you desire, written in the present tense as if it has already happened.

To create a vision for your financial future, take some time to imagine your ideal financial situation. Picture yourself living the life you desire, free from financial stress and worry. What does this life look like? What kind of lifestyle are you living? How are you spending your time? Write down your vision in as much detail as possible, using specific, concrete language.

Once you have a clear vision of your financial future, you can use it to guide your goal-setting process. Your vision becomes the North Star that helps you stay focused and motivated, even when obstacles arise.

The Power of a Clear Vision for Your Financial Future

The path to financial abundance begins with a clear vision of what you want to achieve. When you have a clear idea of your financial goals and dreams, you can create a plan to make them a reality. Without a clear vision, you may find yourself feeling lost or stuck, unsure of which direction to take.

Visualizing your financial future is a powerful tool that can help you create the life you desire. It allows you to tap into the creative power of your mind, helping you to manifest your dreams into reality. With the right mindset and techniques, you can harness the power of visualization to achieve financial abundance.

One of the first steps in creating a clear vision for your financial future is to identify your values and priorities. Ask yourself what matters most to you, what brings you joy and fulfillment, and what you want to achieve in life. From there, you can set specific financial goals that align with your values and vision.

Once you have identified your financial goals, it is important to create a detailed plan for achieving them. This plan should include specific actions and milestones, as well as a timeline for achieving each goal. It may also be helpful to enlist the support of a financial advisor or coach who can help you create a realistic plan for achieving your goals.

Visualization techniques can be a powerful tool for bringing your financial goals to life. Begin by setting aside time each day to focus on your financial goals and dreams. Close your eyes and imagine yourself already living the life you desire. Visualize yourself achieving your financial goals, feeling the sense of accomplishment and satisfaction that comes with success.

Another effective visualization technique is to create a vision board. A vision board is a collage of images and words that represent your financial goals and dreams. It can include pictures of your dream home, your ideal job, or the places you want to travel. By placing your vision board where you can see it every day, you can keep your financial goals at the forefront of your mind, helping you to stay motivated and focused on achieving them.

Remember that the key to successful visualization is to focus on the feelings associated with achieving your financial goals, rather than just the material possessions or achievements themselves. Focus on the sense of abundance, freedom, and joy that comes with financial success, rather than just the dollar amount in your bank account.

By setting clear financial goals and harnessing the power of visualization, you can create a clear vision for your financial future and begin taking the steps to make it a reality. With intention, focus, and perseverance, you can achieve financial abundance and live the life you desire.

How to Align Your Actions with Your Financial Intentions

Once you have set your goals and have a clear vision for your financial future, it's essential to align your actions with your intentions. This chapter will discuss some strategies for doing just that.

1. Create a financial plan: Creating a financial plan is the first step in aligning your actions with your intentions. A financial plan helps you organize your finances and keep track of your progress towards your goals. When creating a financial plan, you should consider your current financial situation, your financial goals, and the steps you need to take to achieve those goals. A financial plan can also help you identify areas where you may need to make changes to your spending habits.

2. Review your budget: Your budget is a critical part of your financial plan. It's essential to review your budget regularly to ensure that you're sticking to it and making progress towards your financial goals. If you find that you're not sticking to your budget, it may be time to make some changes. Reviewing your budget regularly can also help you identify areas where you can cut back on expenses to free up more money to put towards your financial goals.

3. Stay mindful of your spending: Mindful spending means being intentional about the money you spend. When you're mindful of your spending, you're more likely to make choices that align with your financial goals. Before making a purchase, ask yourself if it's something you really need, or if

it's something that will bring you closer to your financial goals. If it's not necessary, consider holding off on the purchase until you have more money to spare.

4. Automate your savings: Automating your savings is a great way to ensure that you're making progress towards your financial goals. By setting up automatic transfers from your checking account to your savings account, you can save money without even thinking about it. This can help you build up your emergency fund or save for a big financial goal like a down payment on a home.

5. Seek support: Finally, it's essential to seek support as you work towards your financial goals. This could mean working with a financial planner or coach, joining a support group of like-minded individuals, or simply talking to friends and family about your goals. Having support can help keep you accountable and motivated to stick to your financial plan.

Aligning your actions with your financial intentions is crucial if you want to achieve financial success. Creating a financial plan, reviewing your budget regularly, staying mindful of your spending, automating your savings, and seeking support are all strategies that can help you stay on track towards your goals. Remember that building wealth takes time, patience, and commitment, but with a clear vision and intentional actions, you can achieve financial success.

Overcoming Limiting Beliefs About Money

Identifying Your Limiting Beliefs

Beliefs are the foundation of our thoughts, actions, and decisions. They shape our reality, influencing how we perceive and respond to the world around us. Some beliefs, however, can be limiting, holding us back from achieving our true potential. These limiting beliefs can be deeply ingrained, passed down from family members, cultural or societal conditioning, or past experiences.

Limiting beliefs can manifest in various areas of our lives, including our relationships, career, and finances. In terms of finances, limiting beliefs can create obstacles that prevent us from achieving our financial goals and attaining financial freedom. These beliefs can create negative self-talk, feelings of unworthiness, and a lack of confidence in our ability to manage money and build wealth.

One common limiting belief about money is that "money is the root of all evil." This belief stems from a misinterpretation of a biblical verse which actually states that "the love of money is the root of all kinds of evil." This belief can lead individuals to subconsciously sabotage their own financial success or feel guilty for pursuing wealth. Another limiting belief is that "rich people are greedy and selfish," which can create a fear of wealth and prevent individuals from taking risks that could lead to financial abundance.

Identifying limiting beliefs is the first step in overcoming them. To do this, it is helpful to reflect on past experiences, messages received from family and friends, and cultural conditioning. Examining our self-talk can also reveal any limiting beliefs we may hold. For example, if we find ourselves saying things like "I'm not good with money" or "I'll never be able to afford that," it may be an indication of a limiting belief.

Once we have identified our limiting beliefs, we can work to reframe them and replace them with more positive and empowering beliefs. This involves questioning the validity of the belief, challenging the evidence that supports it, and consciously choosing a new, more empowering belief to replace it. Affirmations and visualization techniques can also be helpful in reinforcing positive beliefs.

In addition to reframing limiting beliefs, it is important to take action towards our financial goals. This may involve learning new financial skills, seeking guidance from a financial advisor, or taking calculated risks that align with our intentions. As we take action and experience successes, we can further reinforce our positive beliefs and build momentum towards financial abundance.

Overall, identifying and reframing limiting beliefs is an important step in achieving financial success and living a fulfilling life. By taking a conscious and intentional approach to our beliefs and actions, we can overcome obstacles and create a new, empowering financial reality.

How to Challenge and Overcome Negative Money Mindsets

Money mindsets, like any mindset, are deeply ingrained in our subconscious minds. They are shaped by our beliefs, experiences, and cultural influences. Negative money mindsets can manifest as limiting beliefs that hinder our ability to achieve financial success and abundance. However, with awareness and a willingness to challenge and shift these mindsets, it is possible to overcome them and cultivate a positive money mindset.

The first step in challenging negative money mindsets is to identify them. This can be done through introspection and self-reflection. Pay attention to your thoughts and feelings around money. Are they positive or negative? Do you feel abundant or scarce? Are you focused on lack or abundance? Once you have identified your negative money mindsets, you can begin to challenge them.

One common negative money mindset is the belief that money is scarce and difficult to come by. This belief can be deeply ingrained and can cause a person to hold on to their money tightly, even to the point of hoarding it. To challenge this mindset, it is important to shift your focus from lack to abundance. One way to do this is to cultivate a mindset of gratitude. Practice gratitude for the money you have, no matter how small, and trust that more abundance will flow to you.

Another common negative money mindset is the belief that money is the root of all evil or that wealthy people are inherently greedy and selfish. This mindset can cause a person to feel guilty or ashamed for wanting financial success, or to sabotage their own financial progress out of a fear of becoming a "bad" person. To challenge this mindset, it is important to recognize that money is simply a tool that can be used for good or bad. Wealthy people are not inherently greedy or selfish, just as poor people are not inherently virtuous or noble. Instead, focus on the positive impact that financial success can have on your life and the lives of others.

A third common negative money mindset is the belief that money is tied to self-worth. This mindset can cause a person to equate their financial success with their personal value and to feel like a failure if they are not earning enough or accumulating wealth at a fast enough pace. To challenge this mindset, it is important to recognize that your worth as a person is not tied to your financial status. You are inherently valuable and deserving of abundance, regardless of your bank account balance. Instead, focus on building a positive relationship with money based on your own values and priorities.

Once you have identified and challenged your negative money mindsets, it is important to replace them with positive, empowering beliefs. This can be done through affirmations, visualization, and other mindset-shifting practices. For example, you might repeat affirmations such as "I am worthy of financial abundance" or "Money flows to me easily and effortlessly". Visualize yourself achieving your financial goals and feeling a sense of peace, joy, and abundance as you do so.

Negative money mindsets can be a major obstacle to achieving financial success and abundance. However, with awareness and a willingness to challenge and shift these mindsets, it is possible to cultivate a positive money mindset that empowers you to create the financial future you desire. By identifying your limiting beliefs and replacing them with positive, empowering beliefs, you can transform your relationship with money and attract more abundance into your life.

The Benefits of Letting Go of Limiting Beliefs

Our beliefs about money and wealth can have a significant impact on our financial well-being. Often, we hold on to limiting beliefs that prevent us from achieving our financial goals and reaching our full potential. These beliefs can come from a variety of sources such as family, culture, religion, and personal experiences. It is important to identify and challenge these limiting beliefs in order to create a positive and abundant mindset towards money.

Limiting beliefs can take many forms, such as:

- "Money is the root of all evil"
- "Money can't buy happiness"
- "I am not good with money"
- "I will always be in debt"
- "I don't deserve to be wealthy"

These beliefs can hold us back and prevent us from taking necessary steps towards financial success. However, letting go of these beliefs can have numerous benefits.

Firstly, letting go of limiting beliefs can increase our confidence in managing our finances. When we believe that we are capable of achieving financial success, we are more likely to take positive actions towards our goals.

We become more willing to learn new financial skills and strategies that can help us make informed decisions about our money.

Secondly, letting go of limiting beliefs can improve our overall mindset towards money. When we let go of negative beliefs and adopt a positive and abundant mindset, we are more likely to attract wealth and abundance into our lives. Our focus shifts from scarcity to abundance, and we start to see opportunities for financial growth and prosperity.

Thirdly, letting go of limiting beliefs can improve our relationships with money and those around us. When we believe that money is a tool for good and that we can use it to make a positive impact, we are more likely to be generous and charitable towards others. We also become more open to receiving abundance from others, which can further increase our financial prosperity.

To let go of limiting beliefs, it is important to identify them and challenge them with positive affirmations and actions. For example, if you believe that you are not good with money, challenge that belief by taking a financial education course or seeking the advice of a financial professional. If you believe that you will always be in debt, challenge that belief by creating a budget and taking steps to pay off your debts.

Letting go of limiting beliefs can have a profound impact on our financial well-being and overall mindset towards money. By identifying and challenging these beliefs, we can create a positive and abundant mindset that attracts financial success and prosperity into our lives.

Building Financial Confidence and Self-Esteem

The Connection Between Financial Confidence and Self-Esteem

The way we view money can have a significant impact on our self-esteem and overall sense of confidence. For many of us, our financial situation is tied to our sense of self-worth, and we may feel ashamed or embarrassed if we don't have as much money as we think we should. Conversely, having financial stability and success can boost our confidence and make us feel more capable and empowered in other areas of our lives.

It's important to recognize that our self-worth is not tied to our net worth. Money is just one aspect of our lives, and there are many other factors that contribute to our value as individuals. However, it can be challenging to separate our sense of self from our financial situation, especially in a society that places so much emphasis on wealth and material success.

One way to build financial confidence and improve our self-esteem is to focus on our financial strengths and successes, no matter how small they may be. It's easy to get caught up in what we don't have or what we haven't achieved, but taking the time to recognize and celebrate our financial wins can help us feel more capable and competent.

Another way to boost our financial confidence is to educate ourselves about money and financial management. When we understand the basics of personal finance and feel in control of our money, we're more likely to feel confident and empowered in our financial decisions. This can help us avoid common pitfalls like overspending or taking on too much debt.

It's also important to be mindful of the messages we receive from society about money and success. We're often bombarded with images of wealthy and successful people, which can create unrealistic expectations and a sense of inadequacy if we don't measure up. By focusing on our own values and priorities, and recognizing that financial success is just one aspect of a fulfilling life, we can cultivate a more balanced and healthy relationship with money.

In summary, our self-worth is not tied to our financial situation, but it's important to recognize the impact that money can have on our sense of confidence and empowerment. By focusing on our financial strengths, educating ourselves about money management, and being mindful of societal messages about wealth and success, we can build financial confidence and improve our overall sense of self-worth.

Strategies for Building Financial Confidence

Financial confidence is the belief in one's ability to manage their finances successfully. It is a crucial aspect of financial well-being and can have a significant impact on one's overall self-esteem. In this chapter, we will discuss some strategies that can help build financial confidence, allowing individuals to take control of their financial lives and make better decisions.

1. Develop a clear understanding of your finances: The first step in building financial confidence is to develop a clear understanding of your financial situation. This includes creating a budget, tracking your expenses, and understanding your income and expenses. It's essential to be aware of your financial status to make informed decisions and set achievable financial goals.

2. Educate yourself: Another important strategy for building financial confidence is education. Learning about personal finance can help individuals make informed decisions and avoid costly mistakes. There are many resources available, such as books, podcasts, and online courses, that can provide valuable information on personal finance topics.

3. Start small: Building financial confidence can be a daunting task, but starting small can help. Begin by setting achievable financial goals, such as paying off a small debt or saving a specific amount of money each month. Accomplishing these goals can give a sense of accomplishment and motivate individuals to take on more significant financial challenges.

4. Seek advice from professionals: Financial advisors can provide guidance and support, particularly when it comes to more complex financial decisions. Working with a financial advisor can provide individuals with the knowledge and confidence needed to make informed decisions about investments, retirement planning, and other financial matters.

5. Practice mindfulness: Mindfulness practices, such as meditation and deep breathing, can help reduce stress and anxiety related to financial matters.

When individuals are calm and focused, they can approach financial decisions with clarity and confidence. Mindfulness can also help individuals avoid impulsive financial decisions made in response to emotional triggers.

6. Celebrate successes: When individuals reach financial goals or make positive financial decisions, it's essential to celebrate these successes. Celebrating financial achievements can provide a sense of pride and accomplishment, reinforcing the belief that one can successfully manage their finances.

Building financial confidence is a gradual process that requires patience, perseverance, and education. By taking steps to improve their understanding of personal finance, seeking advice from professionals, practicing mindfulness, and celebrating successes, individuals can build the confidence needed to take control of their financial lives and achieve their goals. Ultimately, financial confidence can lead to a sense of empowerment and improved self-esteem, providing individuals with the tools needed to create a more fulfilling life.

Tips for Boosting Your Financial Self-Esteem

Your self-esteem plays a crucial role in your financial life. When you feel good about yourself, you tend to make better financial decisions, take calculated risks, and are more willing to invest in yourself and your future. In contrast, low self-esteem can lead to financial stress, poor decisions, and a general sense of lack and scarcity. If you struggle with low financial self-esteem, don't worry, you're not alone. The good news is that there are practical and spiritual strategies you can use to boost your confidence and create a healthier relationship with money.

1. Practice Gratitude: One of the most effective ways to increase your self-esteem is by practicing gratitude. Take a few minutes every day to think about all the things you're grateful for in your life, including your financial situation. Even if you're not where you want to be yet, focus on the progress you've made and the steps you're taking to achieve your financial goals. Celebrate your wins, no matter how small they may seem.

2. Surround Yourself with Positive Influences: Your environment has a significant impact on your self-esteem, including your financial self-esteem. Surround yourself with people who support your financial goals and aspirations. Seek out mentors, coaches, or friends who are knowledgeable and positive about money. Avoid negative influences that make you feel inferior or unworthy. Remember, you are the average of the five people you spend the most time with.

3. Educate Yourself: Knowledge is power when it comes to finances. The more you know about money, the more confident and empowered you'll feel. Make it a priority to educate yourself on financial topics that interest you, whether it's budgeting, investing, or retirement planning. Attend workshops, read books, or take online courses to deepen your knowledge and gain new skills.

4. Track Your Progress: It's essential to track your financial progress regularly. Create a budget and

track your spending to understand where your money is going. Check your credit score and monitor your debt to see how you're improving over time. Celebrate your progress, and use setbacks as an opportunity to learn and grow. By tracking your progress, you'll build confidence and feel more in control of your financial situation.

5. Practice Self-Care: Your physical and emotional health are closely tied to your financial well-being. Practice self-care by getting enough sleep, exercising regularly, and eating a healthy diet. Take time for yourself to recharge, whether it's through meditation, yoga, or a relaxing bath. By taking care of yourself, you'll feel better about yourself, and that positive energy will translate to your financial life.

6. Use Positive Affirmations: Affirmations are a powerful tool for boosting your self-esteem. Create affirmations that support your financial goals and repeat them to yourself every day. For example, "I am capable of achieving my financial goals" or "I am worthy of financial abundance." By focusing on positive affirmations, you'll start to believe in yourself and your ability to create the financial future you desire.

7. Take Action: Finally, take action towards your financial goals. Procrastination and inaction can lead to feelings of inadequacy and low self-esteem. Break down your goals into smaller, actionable steps, and take action every day towards achieving them. By taking consistent action, you'll build momentum and create positive habits that support your financial well-being.

Boosting your financial self-esteem requires a combination of practical and spiritual strategies. By practicing gratitude, surrounding yourself with positive influences, educating yourself, tracking your progress, practicing self-care, using positive affirmations, and taking action towards your goals, you'll create a healthy relationship with money and feel more confident in your financial future. Remember, you are worthy

Living in Alignment with Your Financial Values

Identifying Your Financial Values

Money holds a unique position in our lives as it touches on so many aspects of our existence. It has the power to shape our decisions, influence our relationships, and determine our sense of self-worth. It is not just about the numbers in our bank accounts, but the values that we assign to it. Understanding your financial values is an important step towards building a fulfilling and meaningful relationship with money. In this chapter, we will explore the concept of financial values and how to identify them.

What are Financial Values?

Financial values are the beliefs and principles that guide our financial decisions and behaviors. They are the core ideas that define our relationship with money and influence how we use it in our daily lives. These values can be shaped by our upbringing, cultural background, personal experiences, and our goals and aspirations.

Why Identify Your Financial Values?

Identifying your financial values is essential for creating a strong and healthy relationship with money. It allows you to align your financial decisions and behaviors with your core beliefs and principles. It helps you to make conscious and intentional decisions that reflect your values and support your overall wellbeing. When your financial decisions align with your values, you will feel more confident and empowered in your financial life.

How to Identify Your Financial Values

Identifying your financial values requires a deep reflection on your beliefs, attitudes, and behaviors around money. Here are some steps to help you get started:

1. Reflect on your upbringing and cultural background. Our beliefs and values around money are often shaped by our family and cultural experiences. Reflect on how money was discussed and used in your family and community.
2. Consider your personal experiences with money. Think about how money has impacted your life so far. Have you experienced financial struggles or successes? How have these experiences shaped your beliefs and values around money?
3. Identify your goals and aspirations. What are your long-term financial goals? What are your priorities when it comes to spending and saving money? What kind of lifestyle do you want to lead?
4. Reflect on your spending habits. Look at your spending habits and identify any patterns or themes. Do you spend money on things that align with your values? Are there any areas where you feel like you are overspending or underspending?
5. Ask yourself what money means to you. Think about what money represents to you beyond just a means of exchange. Does it represent security, freedom, power, or something else?

6. Write down your financial values. Based on your reflection, identify the core beliefs and principles that guide your financial decisions and behaviors. Write them down and refer to them regularly.

Identifying your financial values is an important step towards building a fulfilling and meaningful relationship with money. It allows you to align your financial decisions and behaviors with your core beliefs and principles. By understanding your financial values, you can make conscious and intentional decisions that support your overall wellbeing and contribute to a more meaningful and purposeful life.

How to Live in Alignment with Your Values

Living in alignment with your values is a crucial component of a fulfilling life, including financial well-being. When your financial decisions align with your values, you can feel a sense of purpose and meaning in your financial goals and actions.

Identifying Your Financial Values

Your financial values are the principles and beliefs that guide your financial decisions. Identifying these values can help you create a financial plan that aligns with your goals and supports your overall well-being. Here are some steps to help you identify your financial values:

1. Reflect on your past financial decisions: Think about the financial decisions you've made in the past and what motivated them. Did you prioritize

saving for the future or spending on experiences in the present? Did you prioritize giving to charitable causes or investing in your education or personal growth?

2. Consider your life priorities: What matters most to you in life? Do you value stability and security, or do you prioritize growth and new experiences? Do you place a high value on family and relationships, or do you prioritize independence and self-care?

3. Examine your beliefs about money: What beliefs do you hold about money, wealth, and success? Do you believe that money is a scarce resource or that abundance is possible for everyone? Do you believe that financial success requires sacrifice or that it is possible to achieve financial success while maintaining a balanced and fulfilling life?

Living in Alignment with Your Values

Once you have identified your financial values, the next step is to live in alignment with them. Here are some tips for doing so:

1. Make conscious financial decisions: Before making a financial decision, take the time to consider whether it aligns with your values. Ask yourself, "Will this decision help me achieve my financial goals and live in alignment with my values?"

2. Create a financial plan: A financial plan is a roadmap for achieving your financial goals in alignment with your values. It can help you prioritize your spending and saving, and ensure

that your financial decisions support your long-term goals.

3. Review your finances regularly: Regularly reviewing your finances can help you stay on track with your financial goals and ensure that your spending aligns with your values. It can also help you identify areas where you may need to make adjustments to better align with your values.

4. Find support: Surround yourself with people who share your values and can provide support and encouragement as you work towards your financial goals. Consider working with a financial advisor who can help you create a financial plan that aligns with your values.

Living in alignment with your financial values is a key component of financial well-being. By identifying your financial values and making conscious financial decisions that align with them, you can create a fulfilling financial life that supports your overall well-being. Remember that financial success is not just about accumulating wealth; it's about creating a life that is in alignment with your values and supports your overall well-being.

The Benefits of Living a Value-Driven Financial Life

Living a value-driven financial life is not only about achieving financial stability or accumulating wealth, but it is also about finding purpose and fulfillment in your financial decisions. When you align your financial goals with your personal values, you can create a life that is both prosperous and meaningful.

One of the primary benefits of living a value-driven financial life is the increased sense of purpose and fulfillment that comes with it. By focusing on your values, you can use your financial resources to support causes that you care about, such as charitable organizations, environmental initiatives, or education programs. This can give you a sense of purpose and make you feel like you are making a positive impact on the world.

Another benefit is increased self-awareness and personal growth. When you take the time to identify your values and align your financial decisions with them, you are forced to examine your priorities and beliefs. This can lead to a deeper understanding of yourself and your motivations, which can help you make more intentional and fulfilling choices in all areas of your life.

Living a value-driven financial life can also help you create a more stable and secure financial future. When you make financial decisions based on your values, you are less likely to make impulsive purchases or get into debt for things that do not align with your priorities. This can lead to a more disciplined and strategic approach to managing your finances, which can ultimately lead to greater financial stability and security.

In addition to these benefits, living a value-driven financial life can also help you feel more content and satisfied with your life. By focusing on your values and using your financial resources to support them, you are more likely to feel fulfilled and purposeful in your daily life. This can lead to a greater sense of contentment and happiness overall.

Overall, living a value-driven financial life is about more than just accumulating wealth or achieving financial stability. It is about finding purpose and fulfillment in your financial decisions, and using your resources to support causes that you care about. By aligning your financial goals with your personal values, you can create a life that is both prosperous and meaningful, and experience a greater sense of purpose, fulfillment, and contentment as a result.

The Importance of Money Mindset in Business

How a Strong Money Mindset Can Benefit Your Business

Running a successful business requires more than just a great product or service. It requires a strong mindset that is focused on growth, abundance, and success. This is especially true when it comes to money. A strong money mindset can make all the difference in the success of your business. In this chapter, we will explore how having a strong money mindset can benefit your business and offer tips for cultivating a mindset that supports financial abundance.

The Importance of a Strong Money Mindset

A strong money mindset is essential for any business owner who wants to build a thriving, sustainable business. When you have a positive relationship with money, you are more likely to make smart financial decisions that support your business's growth and profitability. This includes investing in your business, managing your cash flow effectively, and making strategic financial decisions that help you achieve your goals.

Having a strong money mindset also helps you stay focused and motivated when faced with challenges or setbacks. When you believe that you are capable of achieving financial success, you are more likely to persevere through tough times and come out stronger on the other side. This resilience is a critical trait for any business owner, as setbacks are inevitable in the world of entrepreneurship.

Tips for Cultivating a Strong Money Mindset

If you want to cultivate a strong money mindset that supports your business's success, there are several things you can do. Here are some tips to get you started:

1. Identify your limiting beliefs about money: The first step in cultivating a strong money mindset is to identify any limiting beliefs that may be holding you back. These might include beliefs like "money is evil," "I don't deserve to be wealthy," or "there's never enough money to go around." Once you've identified these beliefs, you can begin to challenge them and replace them with more positive, empowering beliefs.

2. Focus on abundance: Instead of thinking in terms of scarcity (i.e., there's never enough money), focus on abundance. Believe that there is always enough money to go around, and that you can attract financial abundance into your life and your business.

3. Set clear financial goals: Setting clear financial goals for your business is essential for cultivating a strong money mindset. When you have specific goals to work toward, you are more likely to stay motivated and focused on achieving financial success.

4. Practice gratitude: Gratitude is a powerful tool for cultivating a positive money mindset. Take time each day to reflect on the things you are grateful for in your business and your life, including your financial successes and opportunities.

5. Surround yourself with positivity: Surrounding yourself with positivity and like-minded people can also help you cultivate a strong money mindset. Seek out mentors, peers, and other business owners who share your values and goals, and who can offer support and encouragement along the way.

A strong money mindset is essential for any business owner who wants to build a successful, sustainable business. By cultivating a positive relationship with money, focusing on abundance, setting clear financial goals, practicing gratitude, and surrounding yourself with positivity, you can create a mindset that supports financial abundance and success. Remember, building a strong money mindset takes time and effort, but the rewards are well worth it. With the right mindset, you can achieve financial success and build a business that supports your goals, values, and vision.

The Connection Between Mindset and Business Success

The world of business can be highly competitive, with everyone vying for their piece of the pie. While many factors come into play when it comes to success, there is one aspect that often goes overlooked: mindset. Our mindset can play a significant role in our business success, and it's essential to understand the connection between the two.

Our mindset is the collection of beliefs, attitudes, and thoughts we have about ourselves, others, and the world around us. It shapes our perception of reality and how we respond to different situations. In the context of business, having a strong and positive mindset can help you navigate the ups and downs that come with entrepreneurship.

One of the most crucial aspects of a strong mindset in business is resilience. Entrepreneurs face numerous challenges, from financial difficulties to interpersonal conflicts. Having the resilience to bounce back from these setbacks can make all the difference in the success of a business. A strong mindset can help entrepreneurs stay motivated and focused, even in the face of adversity.

Another critical aspect of a strong money mindset in business is the ability to take calculated risks. Business success often requires taking risks, whether it's investing in a new product or expanding into a new market. A positive mindset can help entrepreneurs assess risks and make informed decisions, leading to more significant rewards.

Having a strong money mindset can also help entrepreneurs cultivate a growth mindset. This means seeing failure as an opportunity for growth and learning, rather than as a personal defeat. Entrepreneurs with a growth mindset are more likely to persist in the face of challenges and come out on top. Finally, a strong money mindset can help entrepreneurs build strong relationships with customers, employees, and partners. By cultivating a positive and abundant mindset, entrepreneurs can create a culture of positivity and collaboration, leading to more significant success in the long run.

A strong money mindset is essential for success in business. It can help entrepreneurs navigate challenges, take calculated risks, cultivate a growth mindset, and build strong relationships. By understanding the connection between mindset and business success, entrepreneurs can take steps to cultivate a positive and abundant mindset, leading to greater success in their ventures.

Tips for Cultivating a Prosperous Mindset in Business

As an entrepreneur, having a prosperous mindset can be a game-changer for your business. The way you approach your business and your life can have a significant impact on your success. Developing a prosperous mindset can help you attract abundance, overcome obstacles, and achieve your business goals. In this chapter, we will explore some tips for cultivating a prosperous mindset in business.

1. Practice Gratitude Gratitude is a powerful tool that can help you shift your focus from what you don't have to what you do have. By focusing on the abundance in your life, you can attract more abundance into your business. Take time each day to reflect on what you're grateful for in your business and your life. This can be as simple as writing down three things you're grateful for each morning.

2. Focus on Abundance Instead of dwelling on scarcity, focus on abundance. Believe that there is enough to go around, and that opportunities are abundant. Focus on the possibilities and opportunities that exist in your business, rather than the challenges and obstacles. This mindset

shift can help you attract more abundance and success into your business.

3. Believe in Yourself Believing in yourself is essential to cultivating a prosperous mindset. Believe that you have the skills and abilities to succeed in your business. When self-doubt creeps in, remind yourself of your past successes and accomplishments. Celebrate your wins, no matter how small they may be, and use them as fuel to keep moving forward.

4. Embrace Challenges Challenges are an inevitable part of entrepreneurship. Instead of fearing challenges, embrace them as opportunities for growth and learning. When faced with a challenge, ask yourself what you can learn from the experience. Look for the silver lining in difficult situations, and use the lessons learned to improve your business.

5. Surround Yourself with Positive People The people you surround yourself with can have a significant impact on your mindset and success. Surround yourself with positive, like-minded individuals who support and encourage you. Seek out mentorship and guidance from those who have achieved the success you desire. Join networking groups and communities of entrepreneurs who share your values and mindset.

6. Visualize Success Visualization is a powerful tool that can help you achieve your business goals. Take time each day to visualize your business success. Imagine yourself achieving your goals, and feel the emotions associated with that success. Use visualization as a tool to keep you motivated and focused on your goals.

Cultivating a prosperous mindset is essential to business success. By practicing gratitude, focusing on abundance, believing in yourself, embracing challenges, surrounding yourself with positive people, and visualizing success, you can develop a prosperous mindset that attracts abundance and success into your business. Remember, your mindset is a choice, so choose prosperity and watch your business thrive.

The Role of Gratitude in Business Success

How Gratitude Can Benefit Your Business

Gratitude is a powerful tool that can have a profound impact on all aspects of our lives, including our businesses. It is easy to get caught up in the day-to-day struggles of running a business, but taking time to express gratitude can help us maintain perspective and focus on the positive aspects of our work. In this chapter, we will explore how gratitude can benefit your business and provide practical tips for incorporating gratitude into your daily routine.

Gratitude and Business Success:

Research has shown that gratitude can have a significant impact on business success. One study found that companies with a culture of gratitude have higher employee retention rates and are more likely to achieve their financial goals. Additionally, expressing gratitude towards customers can increase their loyalty and willingness to refer new business. When we take the time to appreciate what we have, we open ourselves up to new opportunities and possibilities.

Practical Tips for Incorporating Gratitude into Your Business:

1. Start a gratitude journal: Set aside time each day to reflect on the things you are grateful for in your business. Write down specific instances where you felt grateful for a particular client, employee,

or success. This will help you stay focused on the positive aspects of your work.

2. Express gratitude to your employees: Take the time to thank your employees for their hard work and dedication. A simple thank you note or expression of appreciation can go a long way in creating a positive and supportive work environment.

3. Thank your customers: Show your customers that you appreciate their business by sending a personalized thank you note or offering a special discount. This will not only strengthen your relationship with existing customers but also encourage new business.

4. Practice gratitude in meetings: Begin meetings by expressing gratitude for a recent success or accomplishment. This will help set a positive tone for the rest of the meeting and encourage collaboration and teamwork.

5. Volunteer in the community: Giving back to the community can help create a sense of gratitude and purpose within your business. Volunteer at a local charity or donate a portion of your profits to a cause you care about.

Incorporating gratitude into your business can have a powerful impact on your success and overall happiness. By taking the time to appreciate the positive aspects of your work and expressing gratitude towards your employees and customers, you can create a supportive and fulfilling work environment. By incorporating these practical tips into your daily routine, you can cultivate a prosperous and grateful mindset in your business.

The Connection Between Gratitude and Business Prosperity

The power of gratitude has been recognized by many ancient traditions and modern science as a key ingredient for living a fulfilling and prosperous life. In recent years, the concept of gratitude has gained popularity in the business world as well, as more and more entrepreneurs and business leaders are realizing the impact it can have on their success.

At its core, gratitude is about acknowledging the positive things in your life, no matter how small they may be. By doing so, you shift your focus away from what's lacking and towards what's already present. This shift in perspective can have a profound impact on your thoughts, feelings, and actions, both personally and professionally.

When it comes to business, gratitude can benefit you in several ways. Firstly, it helps you stay motivated and focused on the things that matter. In the fast-paced and often stressful world of entrepreneurship, it's easy to get caught up in the daily grind and lose sight of the bigger picture. Practicing gratitude can help you stay grounded and remind you of why you started your business in the first place.

Secondly, gratitude can help you build stronger relationships with your team, clients, and customers. When you express gratitude towards others, you show them that you value and appreciate them, which can lead to increased loyalty, trust, and respect. This can translate into higher employee retention rates, more repeat business, and a better reputation in your industry.

Thirdly, gratitude can help you attract more abundance into your business. When you focus on what you already have and express gratitude for it, you send a powerful message to the universe that you are open to receiving more. This can manifest in the form of new opportunities, partnerships, clients, or even financial abundance.

Lastly, practicing gratitude can improve your overall well-being and reduce stress levels. As a business owner, it's easy to get caught up in the never-ending to-do list and constant pressure to perform. Gratitude can help you find moments of joy and appreciation amidst the chaos, which can have a positive impact on your mental and emotional health.

In summary, there is a strong connection between gratitude and business prosperity. By cultivating a mindset of gratitude, you can stay motivated, build stronger relationships, attract more abundance, and improve your well-being. Incorporating daily gratitude practices into your business routine can be a powerful way to stay aligned with your values and create a fulfilling and prosperous business.

Tips for Cultivating a Grateful Business Mindset

Gratitude is a powerful emotion that has the ability to transform our lives in many ways, including our businesses. When we cultivate a grateful mindset, we are more likely to attract success and prosperity. We are also more likely to see opportunities and solutions to challenges that we may otherwise miss.

1. Start with Gratitude Journaling

One of the most effective ways to cultivate a grateful mindset is to start a gratitude journal. Take a few minutes each day to write down a few things that you are grateful for in your business. This can be anything from a positive interaction with a client to a successful project completion. By focusing on the positive aspects of your business, you will start to shift your mindset towards gratitude and abundance.

2. Focus on Abundance, Not Scarcity

Many business owners fall into the trap of thinking in terms of scarcity, rather than abundance. They worry about competition, scarcity of resources, and the possibility of failure. However, this mindset only serves to limit their potential for success. Instead, focus on the abundance that surrounds you. Think about the abundance of clients, resources, and opportunities available to you. When you focus on abundance, you are more likely to attract it.

3. Practice Gratitude in Interactions with Others

As a business owner, you likely have interactions with many people throughout the day, including clients, employees, and vendors. Use these interactions as an opportunity to practice gratitude. Express your gratitude to your clients for their business, and to your employees for their hard work. This not only helps to cultivate a grateful mindset but also strengthens your relationships with others.

4. Cultivate a Positive Company Culture

A positive company culture is one that values and encourages gratitude. Make it a point to recognize and celebrate the accomplishments of your employees. Encourage them to express gratitude to each other for their contributions to the team. By cultivating a culture of gratitude, you are not only promoting positivity but also increasing employee satisfaction and retention.

5. Practice Gratitude for Setbacks and Challenges

It can be easy to fall into negativity when faced with setbacks or challenges in your business. However, reframing these experiences as opportunities for growth and learning can help you to maintain a grateful mindset. Reflect on what you have learned from the experience and express gratitude for the opportunity to grow and improve.

6. Celebrate Your Successes

Finally, it is important to celebrate your successes, no matter how small they may seem. Take time to reflect on what you have accomplished and express gratitude for the opportunities that led to your success. Celebrating your successes not only helps to cultivate a grateful mindset but also promotes a sense of accomplishment and motivation.

Cultivating a grateful business mindset is a powerful tool for success and prosperity. By focusing on abundance, practicing gratitude in interactions with others, cultivating a positive company culture, and celebrating your successes, you can shift your mindset towards gratitude and attract more success in your business. Remember, gratitude is a practice, so be patient with yourself as you work to cultivate this mindset in your business.

Creating a Successful Money Mindset in Investing

Understanding the Psychology of Investing

Investing is a complex field that requires both knowledge and a certain level of psychological fortitude. It's important to understand that investing is not just about numbers and data, but it also involves emotions, biases, and personal beliefs. Therefore, having a good understanding of the psychology of investing can help investors make more informed decisions and achieve their financial goals.

One of the most important aspects of the psychology of investing is understanding the concept of risk. Investing always involves risk, whether it's the risk of losing money, the risk of missing out on potential gains, or the risk of making a wrong decision. Investors need to have a clear understanding of the risks involved in their investments and the level of risk they are comfortable with.

Another important aspect of the psychology of investing is the concept of cognitive biases. Cognitive biases are a type of mental shortcut that the brain uses to make decisions more quickly. However, these shortcuts can often lead to irrational and biased decision-making. There are many different types of cognitive biases that can affect investors, such as the confirmation bias, the overconfidence bias, and the anchoring bias. Being aware of these biases and learning to recognize them can help investors make more rational decisions.

Fear and greed are two of the most powerful emotions that can affect investors. Fear can lead investors to sell their investments too quickly, while greed can lead investors to hold onto investments for too long, hoping for greater returns. It's important for investors to recognize these emotions and learn to control them in order to make more rational investment decisions.

Finally, investors need to understand the importance of having a long-term perspective. Investing is not a get-rich-quick scheme, and success often comes from patient and consistent investing over the long term. It's important to have a clear understanding of your investment goals and to stay committed to them, even in the face of short-term market fluctuations.

Strategies for Cultivating a Successful Money Mindset in Investing

The first step in cultivating a successful money mindset in investing is to have a clear understanding of your goals and objectives. It is important to set realistic and measurable goals, such as saving for retirement, buying a home, or starting a business. By having a clear vision of your financial objectives, you can develop an investment plan that aligns with your goals.

Another key strategy is to educate yourself about the investment market. This can involve reading financial books, attending investment seminars, and consulting with financial professionals. By educating yourself about the investment market, you can make informed decisions about which investments to pursue.

It is also important to adopt a patient and disciplined approach to investing. Successful investors understand that investing is a long-term game and that short-term fluctuations are to be expected. By remaining patient and disciplined, you can weather the ups and downs of the market and stay focused on your long-term objectives.

Another important strategy is to practice emotional detachment when investing. This involves making investment decisions based on data and analysis rather than emotions such as fear or greed. By staying detached from emotions and focusing on the facts, you can make rational investment decisions that are aligned with your financial goals.

Finally, it is important to adopt a growth mindset when investing. A growth mindset involves believing in your ability to learn and improve over time. By adopting a growth mindset, you can embrace challenges and setbacks as opportunities for learning and growth. This can help you stay motivated and resilient in the face of investment challenges.

In summary, cultivating a successful money mindset in investing involves having a clear understanding of your financial objectives, educating yourself about the investment market, adopting a patient and disciplined approach, practicing emotional detachment, and adopting a growth mindset. By embracing these strategies, you can approach investing with confidence and success.

Tips for Investing with Confidence and Intention

The key to successful investing is to approach it with confidence and intention.

1. Educate Yourself: One of the most important steps to investing with confidence is to educate yourself. Learn about different types of investments, such as stocks, bonds, mutual funds, and real estate, and how they work. Take the time to research companies and industries you're interested in investing in, and stay up-to-date on market trends and news.

2. Set Clear Goals: Before you start investing, it's essential to have a clear understanding of your financial goals. Are you investing for retirement, saving for a down payment on a house, or building wealth? Knowing your goals will help you make informed decisions about where and how to invest your money.

3. Develop a Strategy: Once you have a clear understanding of your goals, it's time to develop a strategy. Consider your risk tolerance, timeline, and financial situation. Determine how much you can afford to invest and create a plan for diversifying your portfolio.

4. Stay Disciplined: One of the most critical aspects of successful investing is discipline. Stick to your strategy and avoid making impulsive decisions based on market fluctuations or emotions. Don't let fear or greed drive your decisions.

5. Embrace the Long-Term: Investing is a long-term game. Resist the temptation to check your portfolio daily or make frequent changes. Instead, focus on your long-term goals and trust that your strategy will pay off over time.

6. Seek Professional Advice: If you're feeling overwhelmed or unsure about investing, seek professional advice. A financial advisor can help

you develop a strategy that aligns with your goals and risk tolerance.
7. Practice Gratitude: Finally, it's essential to cultivate a mindset of gratitude when it comes to investing. Be grateful for the opportunities you have to invest in your future, and focus on the progress you're making toward your financial goals.

Investing can be an excellent way to build wealth and achieve your financial goals. By approaching it with confidence and intention, and following these tips, you can make informed decisions that align with your goals and financial situation. Remember to stay disciplined, seek professional advice when needed, and practice gratitude for the opportunities investing provides.

Overcoming Fear and Anxiety Around Money

Identifying Your Money Fears and Anxieties

Money is a topic that can stir up intense emotions, and many of us have fears and anxieties surrounding it. These fears and anxieties can be deeply ingrained, and they can have a significant impact on our relationship with money. In this chapter, we will explore some of the most common money fears and anxieties, and we will offer some strategies for identifying and addressing them.

One of the most common money fears is the fear of not having enough. This fear can manifest in many different ways, from worrying about how to pay bills or put food on the table to being afraid of losing a job or experiencing a financial emergency. When we feel like we don't have enough money, we may be more likely to engage in unhealthy financial behaviors like overspending or hoarding money.

Another common money fear is the fear of failure. This fear can be especially pronounced when it comes to investing, where the possibility of losing money can be very real. When we are afraid of failure, we may be hesitant to take risks or try new things, even if they have the potential to benefit us financially.

The fear of judgment is also a significant factor for many people when it comes to money. We may worry about what others will think of us if we don't have a certain amount of money or if we make certain financial decisions. This fear can lead to a lot of pressure and stress around money, and it can be challenging to break free from this cycle.

Identifying your money fears and anxieties is an essential step in overcoming them. To do this, you may want to spend some time reflecting on your past experiences with money and thinking about how those experiences have shaped your beliefs and attitudes. You can also consider seeking out support from a financial advisor or therapist who can help you explore these issues in more depth.

Once you have identified your money fears and anxieties, you can begin to develop strategies for addressing them. This may involve working to reframe your beliefs about money or taking practical steps to reduce financial stress and anxiety. For example, if you are worried about not having enough money, you may want to work on building up an emergency fund or exploring ways to increase your income. If you are afraid of judgment, you may want to work on developing a stronger sense of self-worth and confidence.

Ultimately, the key to addressing money fears and anxieties is to approach them with compassion and curiosity. Rather than judging yourself for feeling anxious or fearful, try to understand where those feelings are coming from and work to develop strategies for overcoming them. By doing so, you can create a more positive and empowering relationship with money that supports your overall financial well-being.

Strategies for Overcoming Fear and Anxiety Around Money

Money fears and anxieties are common among many people. Whether it's the fear of losing money, the anxiety of not having enough, or the worry of making the wrong financial decision, these emotions can create significant barriers to financial success. However, with the right strategies and mindset, it is possible to overcome these fears and anxieties and achieve a healthy relationship with money.

1. Identify Your Money Fears and Anxieties The first step in overcoming money fears and anxieties is to identify what they are. Take some time to reflect on your thoughts and feelings about money. Consider questions such as:

- What are your biggest financial fears?
- What events or situations trigger your money anxieties?
- How do you typically react to financial stress?

By understanding your fears and anxieties, you can begin to work through them and develop strategies for managing them.

2. Practice Mindfulness Mindfulness is the practice of being present in the moment, without judgment or distraction. This technique can be incredibly helpful for managing anxiety and stress related to money. When you feel overwhelmed or anxious about money, take a few deep breaths and focus on the present moment. This can help to calm your mind and reduce your stress levels.

114

3. Educate Yourself One of the best ways to overcome money fears and anxieties is to educate yourself about personal finance. This can include learning about budgeting, investing, and debt management. By understanding the basics of personal finance, you can feel more confident in your financial decision-making and reduce your anxiety.

4. Create a Financial Plan A financial plan can provide a sense of structure and direction when it comes to your finances. It can help you to set goals, prioritize your spending, and manage your debt. By creating a plan, you can feel more in control of your finances and reduce your anxiety.

5. Seek Professional Help If your money fears and anxieties are particularly intense or are negatively impacting your daily life, consider seeking professional help. A therapist or financial advisor can provide guidance and support as you work through your emotions and develop strategies for managing your finances.

Money fears and anxieties can be challenging to overcome, but they do not have to control your life. By identifying your fears, practicing mindfulness, educating yourself, creating a financial plan, and seeking professional help if needed, you can take control of your finances and overcome your anxieties. With time and persistence, you can develop a healthy relationship with money and achieve financial success.

The Benefits of Letting Go of Money-Related Stress

Money-related stress is a common experience for many people, and it can manifest in various ways, including anxiety, fear, and worry. Financial stress can stem from a variety of sources, such as debt, a lack of financial stability, or the pressure to succeed financially. However, letting go of money-related stress can bring significant benefits to one's mental and emotional well-being.

First and foremost, letting go of money-related stress can lead to a greater sense of peace and inner calm. When individuals are constantly worrying about their finances, it can create a sense of unease that permeates their lives. This stress can affect their relationships, their job performance, and their overall quality of life. By releasing this stress, individuals can experience a sense of relief and begin to focus on the positive aspects of their lives.

In addition to improving one's mental and emotional well-being, letting go of money-related stress can also have a positive impact on one's physical health. Studies have shown that financial stress can lead to a variety of physical health problems, including headaches, stomach issues, and even heart disease. By releasing this stress, individuals can improve their overall health and reduce the risk of developing these health problems.

Another benefit of letting go of money-related stress is the ability to make better financial decisions. When individuals are stressed about money, they may make impulsive decisions or avoid making decisions altogether. This can lead to financial mistakes and missed opportunities. By releasing this stress, individuals can think more clearly and make better-informed decisions about their finances.

Moreover, letting go of money-related stress can also lead to increased financial success. When individuals are focused on their financial worries, they may miss out on opportunities or fail to take action that could lead to financial success. By releasing this stress, individuals can focus their energy on creating a positive financial future and taking advantage of opportunities that come their way.

Letting go of money-related stress can have a significant impact on one's overall well-being. It can lead to a greater sense of peace and calm, improved physical health, better financial decision-making, and increased financial success. By identifying and releasing money-related stress, individuals can create a more positive and abundant financial future for themselves.

The Power of Mindset in Wealth Preservation

The Connection Between Mindset and Wealth Preservation

When it comes to wealth preservation, a strong money mindset is essential. How we think and feel about our finances can have a significant impact on our ability to maintain and grow our wealth over time. In this chapter, we will explore the connection between mindset and wealth preservation, and how you can cultivate a mindset that supports your financial goals.

One of the most important aspects of a strong money mindset when it comes to wealth preservation is a focus on long-term thinking. Many people get caught up in the short-term ups and downs of the stock market or other investments, and this can lead to poor decisions that ultimately harm their long-term financial stability. By focusing on the big picture and thinking about how your investments will perform over the long term, you can make better decisions that help to preserve and grow your wealth over time.

Another key aspect of a strong money mindset when it comes to wealth preservation is a willingness to take calculated risks. While it's important to be cautious and thoughtful when making investment decisions, it's also important to recognize that taking calculated risks can be a necessary part of growing your wealth over time. By balancing risk and reward and being willing to take calculated risks when appropriate, you can put yourself in a better position to preserve and grow your wealth over the long term.

In addition to these specific strategies, there are also a number of more general mindset shifts that can be beneficial when it comes to wealth preservation. For example, cultivating a sense of abundance and gratitude can help you to focus on the positive aspects of your financial situation, which in turn can help you to make better decisions and feel more confident about your ability to preserve and grow your wealth.

Another important mindset shift is a focus on continuous learning and growth. The financial world is constantly evolving, and by staying up-to-date on the latest trends and strategies, you can position yourself to make better decisions and preserve your wealth more effectively over time.

Ultimately, the connection between mindset and wealth preservation is a complex and multifaceted one. By focusing on developing a strong money mindset, staying up-to-date on the latest trends and strategies, and being willing to take calculated risks when appropriate, you can put yourself in the best possible position to preserve and grow your wealth over the long term.

Strategies for Preserving Your Wealth

Preserving wealth is an important aspect of personal finance. It involves maintaining and protecting the wealth that one has accumulated over time. Wealth preservation requires careful planning, strategic thinking, and a proactive approach. In this chapter, we will discuss various strategies for preserving wealth and ensuring long-term financial security.

1. Diversification of Assets: Diversification of assets is a fundamental strategy for preserving wealth. It involves spreading investments across different asset classes such as stocks, bonds, real estate, and alternative investments. Diversification helps to reduce the risk of loss and ensures that the portfolio is not overly dependent on one particular investment.

2. Asset Protection Planning: Asset protection planning is another key strategy for preserving wealth. It involves taking steps to protect assets from potential legal claims, lawsuits, or creditor actions. This can be achieved through the use of trusts, limited liability companies, and other legal structures.

3. Estate Planning: Estate planning is essential for preserving wealth across generations. It involves developing a comprehensive plan for the distribution of assets upon death. An effective estate plan should include a will, trust, and other relevant documents to ensure that assets are distributed according to the wishes of the individual.

4. Tax Planning: Tax planning is a critical component of wealth preservation. It involves understanding the tax implications of various financial decisions and taking steps to minimize tax liabilities. Effective tax planning can help to preserve wealth by reducing the amount of taxes paid on investments and other income sources.

5. Long-Term Investment Approach: A long-term investment approach is crucial for preserving

wealth. It involves investing in quality assets with a long-term horizon in mind. This approach can help to mitigate the risks associated with short-term market fluctuations and volatility.

6. Regular Monitoring and Review: Regular monitoring and review of investments and financial plans are essential for preserving wealth. It involves regularly reviewing investment performance, financial goals, and risk tolerance to ensure that the portfolio remains aligned with the individual's objectives and values.

In summary, preserving wealth requires a proactive approach that involves careful planning, strategic thinking, and a long-term perspective. By diversifying assets, engaging in asset protection planning, estate planning, tax planning, adopting a long-term investment approach, and regularly monitoring and reviewing financial plans, individuals can preserve and protect their wealth for future generations.

Tips for Maintaining a Wealth-Preserving Mindset

Maintaining a wealth-preserving mindset is essential for long-term financial success. It involves having a clear understanding of your financial goals, a disciplined approach to managing your finances, and a commitment to making smart financial decisions. In this chapter, we will explore some tips for maintaining a wealth-preserving mindset.

1. Educate Yourself: The first step in maintaining a wealth-preserving mindset is to educate yourself

about finance and investing. Read books and articles, attend seminars and webinars, and seek out advice from financial experts. The more you know about finance and investing, the better equipped you will be to make informed decisions about your money.

2. Develop a Long-Term Strategy: To preserve your wealth, it's important to have a long-term strategy in place. This means setting clear financial goals and developing a plan to achieve them. You should consider your current financial situation, your risk tolerance, and your investment goals when developing your strategy.

3. Diversify Your Investments: One of the keys to preserving your wealth is to diversify your investments. This means spreading your money across different asset classes, such as stocks, bonds, real estate, and commodities. Diversification helps to reduce the risk of losses and can provide a more stable return over the long-term.

4. Stay Disciplined: To maintain a wealth-preserving mindset, it's essential to stay disciplined in your approach to managing your finances. This means sticking to your long-term strategy, avoiding impulsive financial decisions, and staying focused on your financial goals.

5. Be Patient: Building and preserving wealth takes time and patience. It's important to avoid the temptation to make quick money and instead focus on making consistent, long-term gains. Remember that financial success is a marathon, not a sprint.

6. Stay Positive: A positive mindset is essential for maintaining a wealth-preserving mindset. Instead

of focusing on the negatives, such as market fluctuations or economic uncertainty, focus on the positives, such as the long-term potential of your investments. A positive mindset can help you stay committed to your financial goals and maintain a disciplined approach to managing your finances.

7. Seek Professional Advice: Finally, don't be afraid to seek out professional advice when it comes to managing your finances. Financial advisors and wealth managers can provide valuable insights and guidance on how to achieve your financial goals and preserve your wealth over the long-term.

Maintaining a wealth-preserving mindset requires discipline, patience, and a commitment to making smart financial decisions. By educating yourself, developing a long-term strategy, staying disciplined, and maintaining a positive mindset, you can preserve your wealth and achieve long-term financial success.

Creating Financial Abundance through Generosity

The Connection Between Generosity and Financial Abundance

In the pursuit of financial abundance, it is easy to focus solely on accumulating wealth and achieving financial goals. However, it is important to remember that true wealth and abundance come not only from what we receive but also from what we give. Generosity, the act of giving freely and abundantly, can be a powerful tool for attracting financial abundance.

There is a deep spiritual connection between generosity and financial abundance. When we give without expecting anything in return, we create a positive energy that attracts abundance into our lives. This is because generosity is an act of abundance, and it sends a message to the universe that we have enough to share. In turn, the universe responds by sending us more abundance.

Furthermore, generosity helps to shift our mindset from scarcity to abundance. When we give, we are acting from a place of abundance, which helps to dissolve the fears and limiting beliefs that can block financial abundance from flowing into our lives. Generosity also helps to cultivate gratitude, which is another powerful tool for attracting abundance.

Generosity can also have practical benefits for our financial well-being. When we give freely and without expectation, we create positive relationships with others. This can lead to opportunities and connections that can

124

help us to achieve our financial goals. Additionally, giving can help us to feel more connected to our community and to the world around us, which can lead to a greater sense of purpose and fulfillment in our lives.

Overall, the connection between generosity and financial abundance is strong and powerful. By cultivating a mindset of generosity and giving freely and abundantly, we can attract more abundance into our lives and experience greater financial well-being.

How to Cultivate a Generous Mindset

In the world of finance, generosity is often overlooked or undervalued. However, having a generous mindset can actually help you achieve greater financial abundance and success. Generosity is not just about giving away money or material possessions, but it's also about being open, compassionate, and grateful for what you have. In this chapter, we will explore how to cultivate a generous mindset in order to attract more abundance into your life.

1. Practice Gratitude: A generous mindset starts with gratitude. When you appreciate what you have, you are less focused on what you lack. Being grateful for your blessings, whether they are financial or not, can help you shift your focus towards abundance. Start a gratitude journal or practice giving thanks every morning for the things you have in your life.
2. Give to Others: Giving to others can also help cultivate a generous mindset. This doesn't necessarily have to involve money or material possessions. It could be as simple as giving

someone a compliment or a helping hand. Volunteering your time for a charity or cause that you are passionate about is also a great way to give back to your community.

3. Be Open: A generous mindset also involves being open to new opportunities and experiences. This means being willing to take risks and stepping outside of your comfort zone. When you approach life with an open mind, you are more likely to attract new and exciting opportunities into your life.

4. Practice Abundance Mindset: An abundance mindset is the belief that there is enough to go around for everyone. This means letting go of any scarcity or lack mentality that you may have. When you believe that there is an abundance of wealth and opportunity, you are more likely to attract it into your life.

5. Let Go of Greed: Finally, a generous mindset also involves letting go of any greed or attachment to material possessions. This doesn't mean you shouldn't enjoy the things you have, but rather you should be mindful of your relationship with money and material possessions. When you approach wealth with a sense of detachment, you are more likely to attract it into your life.

Cultivating a generous mindset can help you attract more abundance and financial success into your life. By practicing gratitude, giving to others, being open, embracing an abundance mindset, and letting go of greed, you can shift your focus towards abundance and cultivate a mindset of generosity. When you approach life with an open and generous mindset, you will be amazed at the opportunities that come your way.

The Benefits of Giving Back for Financial Prosperity

The act of giving back is a powerful and transformative force that can bring significant benefits to those who practice it, particularly in the realm of financial prosperity. It is a universal principle that giving leads to receiving, and this is especially true when it comes to money.

When we give back, we open ourselves up to a flow of abundance that goes beyond the tangible benefits of wealth. It can bring us a sense of purpose, fulfillment, and happiness that cannot be achieved through material possessions alone. By giving to others, we shift our focus away from our own needs and desires and towards the greater good of the community. This shift in perspective can lead to a sense of interconnectedness with others and a greater appreciation for the abundance that surrounds us.

Moreover, the act of giving can have a profound impact on our financial success. When we give generously, we signal to the universe that we have an abundance mindset and are willing to share our resources with others. This mindset attracts more wealth and abundance into our lives, as we are open and receptive to receiving. By giving to others, we also create a ripple effect of generosity and abundance in the world, as our actions inspire others to give and to create positive change.

In addition to the spiritual benefits of giving, there are also practical benefits that can enhance our financial prosperity. Giving to charitable causes can provide tax benefits and can help us build a network of relationships that can lead to business opportunities or career advancement. Giving can also help us develop a reputation for generosity and integrity, which can enhance our professional standing and make us more attractive to potential clients or investors.

Overall, giving back is a powerful tool for cultivating financial prosperity and abundance. By shifting our focus away from ourselves and towards the greater good, we open ourselves up to a flow of abundance that can bring us both spiritual and practical benefits. When we give generously and with an open heart, we create a positive impact on the world and invite greater prosperity and abundance into our lives.

The Role of Mindset in Career Success

The Connection Between Mindset and Career Success

In today's highly competitive job market, it's more important than ever to have a strong mindset to achieve career success. While skills and education are important, having the right mindset can make all the difference when it comes to landing your dream job, getting a promotion, or achieving success in your chosen field. In this chapter, we will explore the connection between mindset and career success and provide you with practical tips for cultivating a mindset that will help you achieve your professional goals.

The Power of a Positive Mindset

Research has shown that having a positive mindset can have a significant impact on career success. A positive mindset can help you to stay motivated, overcome obstacles, and develop resilience in the face of challenges. It can also help you to build strong relationships with colleagues and clients, which can be crucial in achieving career success.

One of the key benefits of a positive mindset is increased confidence. When you approach your work with a positive outlook, you are more likely to believe in your abilities and take on new challenges with enthusiasm. This confidence can help you to take risks and pursue opportunities that you might have otherwise passed up, leading to greater career success over time.

Another benefit of a positive mindset is improved creativity. When you approach your work with an open mind and a positive attitude, you are more likely to think outside the box and come up with innovative solutions to problems. This can help you to stand out in your field and achieve greater success in your career.

Cultivating a positive mindset is crucial for achieving career success. By practicing gratitude, focusing on solutions, developing a growth mindset, and building strong relationships, you can cultivate a mindset that will help you overcome challenges, take risks, and achieve your professional goals. By approaching your work with a positive outlook and a can-do attitude, you can set yourself up for success and achieve great things in your career.

Strategies for Cultivating a Prosperous Mindset in Your Career

The mind plays a crucial role in shaping the trajectory of one's career. A prosperous mindset can manifest in many ways, such as increased job satisfaction, more significant opportunities for growth, and even financial rewards. Here are some strategies that you can employ to cultivate a prosperous mindset in your career.

1.   Adopt a Growth Mindset:

A growth mindset is one that views challenges as opportunities for growth and learning. It is a belief that one's skills and abilities can be developed through hard work and dedication. Adopting a growth mindset can help you overcome obstacles and navigate setbacks, allowing you to take risks and seize opportunities that will help you achieve your career goals.

2. Focus on Your Strengths:

Identifying your unique strengths and talents can help you build a fulfilling and prosperous career. Focusing on your strengths can help you excel in your work and stand out from the competition. It can also give you a sense of purpose and fulfillment, which can contribute to your overall career success.

3. Develop a Positive Attitude:

A positive attitude is critical in any career. A positive attitude can help you maintain a sense of optimism and resilience in the face of challenges. It can also help you build strong relationships with colleagues and clients, which can lead to new opportunities for growth and advancement.

4. Set Goals and Take Action:

Setting clear, achievable goals is essential for building a prosperous career. Once you have identified your goals, take action towards achieving them. This could mean seeking out new opportunities for growth and development, networking with colleagues in your field, or taking on additional responsibilities at work.

5. Embrace Failure:

Failure is a natural part of any career journey. Embracing failure and viewing it as an opportunity for growth and learning can help you develop resilience and perseverance. It can also help you take risks and pursue opportunities that may lead to significant career rewards.

    6.   Practice Self-Care:

Taking care of your mental and physical health is essential for building a prosperous career. Engaging in activities that help you manage stress, such as exercise or meditation, can help you maintain focus and productivity in your work. It can also contribute to your overall well-being, which is critical for long-term career success.

Cultivating a prosperous mindset in your career requires a combination of self-awareness, goal setting, and positive action. By adopting these strategies, you can build a fulfilling and prosperous career that aligns with your values and goals. Remember to stay focused on your strengths, embrace failure as an opportunity for growth, and prioritize your mental and physical health.

Tips for Achieving Your Professional Goals

Setting professional goals is an essential part of personal and career development. However, it's not enough to merely set goals; it's also important to take action and achieve them. In this chapter, we'll discuss some tips for achieving your professional goals and cultivating a prosperous mindset in your career.

Tip #1: Visualize Your Success

Visualization is a powerful tool for achieving your goals. Take some time to imagine yourself already achieving your professional goals. Imagine how you'll feel, what you'll be doing, and the impact you'll be making. The more you can visualize yourself succeeding, the more likely you are to achieve your goals.

Tip #2: Create a Plan

Having a plan is essential for achieving your professional goals. Start by breaking your goals down into smaller, actionable steps. Then, create a timeline for completing each step. This will help you stay on track and make progress towards your goals.

Tip #3: Take Action

Taking action is the most critical step in achieving your professional goals. Once you have a plan in place, it's time to start taking action. Don't wait for the "perfect" time to start; the perfect time may never come. Instead, take action now and make progress towards your goals every day.

Tip #4: Embrace Failure

Failure is a natural part of the journey towards achieving your goals. Instead of fearing failure, embrace it as an opportunity to learn and grow. Use your failures as feedback to improve your approach and get closer to your goals.

Tip #5: Network and Seek Support

Networking and seeking support from others can be incredibly beneficial in achieving your professional goals. Surround yourself with like-minded individuals who share your values and goals. Seek out mentors and coaches who can provide guidance and support along the way.

Tip #6: Stay Positive and Grateful

Maintaining a positive and grateful mindset is crucial for achieving your professional goals. Focus on the progress you're making, rather than getting discouraged by setbacks. Take time to reflect on what you're grateful for and how far you've come. A positive and grateful mindset will keep you motivated and focused on your goals.

Achieving your professional goals requires a combination of mindset and action. By visualizing your success, creating a plan, taking action, embracing failure, networking, and staying positive and grateful, you can cultivate a prosperous mindset and achieve your professional goals. Remember to be patient, persistent, and focused on your goals, and success will be within reach.

The Benefits of Positive Self-Talk in Financial Success

The Science Behind Positive Self-Talk and Financial Success

The power of positive self-talk has been a topic of interest for many researchers and practitioners. Studies have shown that positive self-talk can improve overall well-being, boost confidence, and lead to greater success in various areas of life, including finances. Positive self-talk can help you develop a more optimistic outlook and cultivate a growth mindset, which can lead to greater financial abundance and prosperity.

The Science Behind Positive Self-Talk: Positive self-talk is a practice that involves consciously directing your thoughts in a positive and empowering way. It involves using affirmations and positive statements to counter negative self-talk and self-doubt. Research has shown that positive self-talk can have a range of benefits for mental health and well-being, including reducing anxiety and depression and improving self-esteem.

Positive self-talk has also been linked to greater success in various areas of life, including finances. A study published in the Journal of Economic Psychology found that people who engaged in positive self-talk about their finances were more likely to make better financial decisions and achieve greater financial success. This is because positive self-talk can help you develop a more optimistic outlook, which can increase your confidence and motivation to take positive action towards your financial goals.

Cultivating a Positive Self-Talk Practice: Cultivating a positive self-talk practice takes time and effort, but the benefits are well worth it. Here are some tips for incorporating positive self-talk into your daily routine:

1. Start by becoming more aware of your self-talk. Notice when you are engaging in negative self-talk and try to reframe those thoughts in a more positive and empowering way.
2. Use affirmations to reinforce positive messages. Create affirmations that align with your financial goals and repeat them to yourself regularly.
3. Surround yourself with positive influences. Seek out mentors, friends, and colleagues who have a positive outlook on life and can help support you in your positive self-talk practice.
4. Practice gratitude. Gratitude is a powerful tool for shifting your mindset towards a more positive outlook. Take time each day to reflect on the things you are grateful for in your life, including your financial abundance.
5. Celebrate your successes. Acknowledge your accomplishments and celebrate your successes, no matter how small they may seem. This can help reinforce positive self-talk and build momentum towards greater financial success.

Positive self-talk can be a powerful tool for improving your financial success and overall well-being. By cultivating a practice of positive self-talk, you can develop a more optimistic outlook and boost your confidence and motivation to achieve your financial goals. Remember to be patient and kind to yourself as you work to develop this practice, and celebrate your successes along the way.

How to Incorporate Positive Self-Talk into Your Money Habits

The way we talk to ourselves can have a profound impact on our thoughts, feelings, and behaviors. Negative self-talk can lead to feelings of self-doubt, anxiety, and even depression. On the other hand, positive self-talk can boost self-confidence, increase motivation, and lead to success. When it comes to money, our self-talk can play a significant role in our financial habits and ultimately our financial success. In this chapter, we will explore how to incorporate positive self-talk into your money habits and the benefits of doing so.

The Power of Positive Self-Talk:

Positive self-talk is the act of consciously choosing to use positive and supportive language when talking to yourself. This can be especially important when it comes to money, as our thoughts and beliefs about money can impact our financial behaviors. When we use positive self-talk, we can shift our mindset from one of scarcity and fear to one of abundance and possibility.

Studies have shown that positive self-talk can have a significant impact on our overall well-being, including our financial health. For example, researchers have found that individuals who engage in positive self-talk are more likely to take action towards achieving their financial goals and are less likely to experience financial stress and anxiety.

Tips for Incorporating Positive Self-Talk into Your Money Habits:

1. Use affirmations: Affirmations are statements that you repeat to yourself to reinforce positive beliefs and attitudes. For example, you might say to yourself, "I am worthy of financial abundance," or "I am capable of achieving my financial goals." Repeat these affirmations regularly, either silently or aloud, to help shift your mindset to one of positivity and possibility.

2. Focus on abundance: Rather than dwelling on what you don't have, focus on what you do have. Take stock of your financial resources and express gratitude for what you have. When you focus on abundance, you will feel more positive and motivated to take action towards your financial goals.

3. Reframe negative thoughts: When negative thoughts creep into your mind, consciously reframe them into positive statements. For example, if you catch yourself thinking, "I'll never be able to save enough for retirement," reframe that thought into something like, "I'm taking steps towards building a secure financial future."

4. Use visualization: Visualization is a powerful tool for reinforcing positive beliefs and behaviors. Close your eyes and imagine yourself achieving your financial goals, whether it's paying off debt, saving for a down payment, or building your retirement nest egg. Visualize yourself succeeding and feeling the sense of accomplishment that comes with achieving your goals.

5. Practice self-compassion: It's important to be kind to yourself as you work towards your financial goals. Recognize that setbacks and challenges are a normal part of the process, and be gentle with yourself when things don't go as planned. Speak

to yourself with the same kindness and compassion that you would offer a friend.

Incorporating positive self-talk into your money habits can have a significant impact on your financial success and overall well-being. By using affirmations, focusing on abundance, reframing negative thoughts, using visualization, and practicing self-compassion, you can cultivate a more positive and supportive mindset when it comes to money. As you continue to incorporate these practices into your daily life, you will begin to see the benefits in the form of increased motivation, confidence, and financial success.

The Benefits of Speaking Positively About Your Finances

The way we talk about our finances can have a significant impact on our financial well-being. Our thoughts and beliefs about money shape our financial behaviors, and the language we use to describe our finances can reinforce those beliefs. Speaking positively about our finances can help us create a more abundant and prosperous financial future. In this chapter, we will explore the benefits of speaking positively about our finances and how it can improve our financial well-being.

1. Increases Confidence

When we speak positively about our finances, it can increase our confidence in our financial decision-making. By speaking positively about our finances, we are affirming our ability to manage our money effectively.

This can help us make more confident financial decisions and take bold steps towards our financial goals.

2. Attracts Abundance

The law of attraction states that like attracts like. When we speak positively about our finances, we are attracting more positive financial energy into our lives. This can manifest in the form of new opportunities, increased income, and unexpected windfalls. By focusing on the abundance in our lives, we are creating a positive financial vibration that attracts more abundance into our lives.

3. Reduces Stress

Talking positively about our finances can also reduce our financial stress levels. When we are constantly worried and anxious about our finances, it can take a toll on our mental and physical health. By speaking positively about our finances, we are reducing the negative impact of financial stress on our lives. This can lead to improved overall well-being and a more positive outlook on life.

4. Increases Gratitude

Speaking positively about our finances can also increase our sense of gratitude. By focusing on the positive aspects of our financial situation, we can cultivate a greater sense of appreciation for what we have. This can help us shift our focus from what we lack to what we have, leading to a more abundant and fulfilling life.

5. Encourages Positive Financial Habits

When we speak positively about our finances, it can also encourage us to develop positive financial habits. By focusing on the positive aspects of our finances, we are more likely to engage in positive financial behaviors, such as saving, investing, and budgeting. This can help us create a more stable and prosperous financial future.

Speaking positively about our finances can have a profound impact on our financial well-being. By increasing our confidence, attracting abundance, reducing stress, increasing gratitude, and encouraging positive financial habits, we can create a more abundant and prosperous financial future. So the next time you talk about your finances, make sure to do it with a positive mindset and watch as your financial abundance grows.

Cultivating Financial Mindfulness in Daily Life

How to Practice Financial Mindfulness in Daily Life

Living in the present moment and being fully aware of one's financial decisions is a crucial component of financial well-being. The practice of financial mindfulness enables individuals to make sound financial decisions, be more conscious of their spending habits, and ultimately achieve their financial goals. In this chapter, we will explore the concept of financial mindfulness and how it can be applied in daily life.

Understanding Financial Mindfulness:

Mindfulness is the practice of being present in the moment and fully aware of one's thoughts, feelings, and surroundings. Financial mindfulness, therefore, is the practice of applying this same level of attention and awareness to one's financial decisions and behaviors. It involves being fully present and aware of one's financial goals, spending habits, and beliefs about money.

Benefits of Financial Mindfulness:

There are numerous benefits to practicing financial mindfulness, including:

1. Improved decision-making: When you are fully present and aware of your financial decisions, you are less likely to make impulsive or emotionally driven purchases. This can lead to better decision-making and ultimately, better financial outcomes.

2. Reduced financial stress: Being mindful of your finances can help reduce financial stress and anxiety. When you have a clear understanding of your financial situation, you are better equipped to make informed decisions and take action to improve your financial well-being.
3. Increased financial satisfaction: Practicing financial mindfulness can help you appreciate the things you have and find contentment in your financial situation. This can lead to a greater sense of financial satisfaction and overall well-being.
4. Improved relationships: Financial mindfulness can also improve your relationships with others. When you are more aware of your spending habits and financial goals, you are better able to communicate them with loved ones and work together towards achieving them.

How to Practice Financial Mindfulness:

1. Set financial goals: Setting clear financial goals is a key component of financial mindfulness. When you have a clear understanding of what you want to achieve, you are better equipped to make decisions that align with those goals.
2. Keep track of your spending: Keeping track of your spending is an important part of financial mindfulness. This can involve tracking your expenses in a budgeting app or simply writing them down in a notebook.
3. Be present in your financial decisions: When making financial decisions, take a moment to pause and reflect on your options. Consider the long-term implications of your decision and how it aligns with your financial goals.

4. Practice gratitude: Practicing gratitude can help cultivate a more mindful approach to your finances. Take time each day to reflect on the things you are grateful for and appreciate the financial resources you have available to you.
5. Avoid comparing yourself to others: Comparing yourself to others can be detrimental to your financial well-being. Instead, focus on your own financial goals and progress and avoid getting caught up in the financial successes of others.

Practicing financial mindfulness is an effective way to improve your financial well-being and achieve your financial goals. By being present and aware of your financial decisions, you can make informed choices, reduce financial stress, and cultivate a greater sense of financial satisfaction. Incorporate the strategies discussed in this chapter into your daily life and start reaping the benefits of financial mindfulness today.

The Connection Between Mindfulness and Financial Well-being

In today's fast-paced world, many people feel overwhelmed and stressed by their financial situation. Whether it's worrying about bills, debt, or retirement savings, money-related stress can have a significant impact on our overall well-being. However, research has shown that practicing mindfulness can help improve our financial well-being and reduce money-related stress. In this chapter, we will explore the connection between mindfulness and financial well-being and how you can apply mindfulness to improve your financial situation.

What is Mindfulness?

Mindfulness is a form of meditation that involves paying attention to the present moment, without judgment. It is the practice of being fully engaged in whatever we are doing, whether that be eating, walking, or working, and noticing our thoughts and feelings without getting caught up in them. Through mindfulness, we learn to observe our thoughts and emotions with curiosity and openness, rather than becoming overwhelmed by them.

The Connection Between Mindfulness and Financial Well-being

Financial stress can have a significant impact on our mental and physical health. It can lead to anxiety, depression, and even physical health problems such as high blood pressure and heart disease. However, practicing mindfulness can help us manage our finances more effectively and reduce money-related stress.

When we are mindful, we are better able to observe our thoughts and emotions around money. This allows us to identify negative patterns and beliefs that may be holding us back from making wise financial decisions. For example, if we notice that we have a belief that money is scarce and difficult to come by, we can challenge that belief and replace it with a more positive and empowering one.

Furthermore, mindfulness helps us stay present in the moment and avoid making impulsive financial decisions. Instead of reacting emotionally to financial situations, we can take a step back and make more thoughtful and deliberate decisions. This can lead to better financial outcomes in the long run.

Practicing mindfulness also helps us develop a sense of abundance and gratitude, which can improve our relationship with money. Instead of focusing on what we lack, we can focus on what we have and cultivate a sense of contentment and fulfillment. This can help us make more conscious spending decisions and avoid overspending or accumulating unnecessary debt.

How to Apply Mindfulness to Your Finances

There are several ways you can apply mindfulness to your finances. Here are some tips to get started:

1. Set aside time for reflection: Take some time each day to reflect on your financial situation. This can be as simple as taking a few minutes to review your bank account or credit card statement, or it can be a more in-depth reflection on your financial goals and priorities.
2. Notice your thoughts and emotions around money: Throughout the day, pay attention to your thoughts and emotions around money. Notice any negative patterns or beliefs that may be holding you back and challenge them with more positive and empowering thoughts.
3. Practice gratitude: Cultivate a sense of gratitude for what you have, rather than focusing on what you lack. Take some time each day to reflect on the blessings in your life and the things you are grateful for.
4. Practice conscious spending: When making financial decisions, take a step back and consider

your options before making a decision. Ask yourself if this purchase aligns with your values and priorities, and if it will bring you true happiness and fulfillment.

5. Practice self-compassion: Finally, remember to be kind and compassionate with yourself as you navigate your finances. Financial well-being is a journey, and there will be ups and downs along the way. Practice self-compassion and celebrate your successes along the way.

Practicing mindfulness can have a significant impact on our financial well-being. By cultivating a mindful approach to our finances, we can reduce money-related stress, make more thoughtful and deliberate financial decisions,

Tips for Living Mindfully with Money

Living mindfully with money is an important aspect of financial well-being. When we are mindful, we are fully present in the moment, aware of our thoughts and actions, and able to make conscious decisions about how we spend and save our money. Mindfulness can help us develop a healthy relationship with money, reduce stress and anxiety related to finances, and improve our overall financial well-being. In this chapter, we will explore some tips for living mindfully with money.

1. Start with awareness: The first step in living mindfully with money is to become aware of your current relationship with money. Take some time to reflect on your thoughts and feelings about money. Are you anxious or stressed about money?

147

Do you feel guilty or ashamed about your spending habits? Understanding your current mindset around money is the first step in cultivating a healthier relationship with your finances.

2. Practice gratitude: Gratitude is an important aspect of mindfulness and can help us develop a more positive relationship with money. Take time each day to reflect on what you are grateful for in your financial life. This can be as simple as feeling thankful for a roof over your head or having food on the table. Focusing on the things you do have can help shift your mindset away from scarcity and towards abundance.

3. Create a budget: Creating a budget is a practical way to live mindfully with money. When you have a budget, you are more aware of your spending habits and can make conscious decisions about how you allocate your money. A budget can also help reduce stress and anxiety related to finances, as you will have a clear picture of where your money is going.

4. Avoid impulsive purchases: Impulsive purchases can be a major obstacle to living mindfully with money. Before making a purchase, take a moment to ask yourself if it aligns with your values and goals. If it doesn't, consider holding off on the purchase and taking some time to reflect on whether it is truly necessary.

5. Use cash: Using cash can be a helpful tool for living mindfully with money. When you use cash, you have a tangible representation of your spending and can be more mindful of how much you are spending. It can also help you avoid overspending and impulse purchases.

6. Practice mindful spending: Mindful spending involves being fully present and aware of your actions when making purchases. Before making a purchase, take a deep breath and ask yourself if it aligns with your values and goals. Consider the long-term impact of the purchase and whether it will bring you joy and satisfaction.

7. Take care of your finances regularly: Regularly checking in on your finances and taking care of them is an important aspect of living mindfully with money. This includes things like paying bills on time, checking your bank account regularly, and reviewing your budget periodically. By taking care of your finances regularly, you can avoid stress and anxiety related to money and feel more in control of your financial situation.

Living mindfully with money involves being aware of your current mindset around money, practicing gratitude, creating a budget, avoiding impulsive purchases, using cash, practicing mindful spending, and taking care of your finances regularly. By incorporating these tips into your daily life, you can develop a healthier relationship with money, reduce stress and anxiety related to finances, and improve your overall financial well-being.

Overcoming Financial Setbacks with Resilience

How to Build Financial Resilience

Building financial resilience is crucial for our well-being and peace of mind. It helps us face unexpected challenges and maintain financial stability in the long run. Financial resilience is not just about having enough savings, but it's also about having a positive mindset and a solid plan to navigate financial difficulties. In this chapter, we'll explore what financial resilience means, why it's important, and how to build it.

What is Financial Resilience? Financial resilience refers to the ability to withstand financial shocks and stressors. It's the ability to bounce back from unexpected financial setbacks, such as job loss, illness, or an economic downturn. Financial resilience is not just about having enough money saved, but it's also about having a solid financial plan and a positive mindset.

Why is Financial Resilience Important? Financial resilience is important for several reasons. First, it helps us maintain financial stability during difficult times. Second, it helps us avoid taking on unnecessary debt or relying on credit cards to cover unexpected expenses. Third, it can reduce stress and anxiety related to money, which can have a significant impact on our overall well-being. Finally, it helps us achieve our long-term financial goals, such as saving for retirement or buying a home.

How to Build Financial Resilience:

1. Build a Solid Emergency Fund: Having an emergency fund is one of the most important steps in building financial resilience. This fund should be enough to cover at least six months' worth of living expenses. Start by setting aside a small portion of your income each month and gradually build up your emergency fund over time. This fund will provide a safety net during difficult times and help you avoid relying on credit cards or loans.

2. Create a Budget: Creating a budget is an essential part of building financial resilience. A budget can help you track your income and expenses and identify areas where you can cut back on spending. This can free up more money to put towards your emergency fund or other financial goals. Stick to your budget as much as possible, and review it regularly to make sure it's still working for you.

3. Pay Off Debt: Paying off debt is another important step in building financial resilience. High levels of debt can be a major source of stress and can make it difficult to weather unexpected financial shocks. Start by paying off high-interest debts first, such as credit card debt or personal loans. This will free up more money to put towards your emergency fund and other financial goals.

4. Diversify Your Income: Diversifying your income can also help you build financial resilience. This means having multiple sources of income, such as a side job or freelance work. If one source of income is affected, you still have other sources to

rely on. This can provide an extra layer of financial security and help you maintain your lifestyle during difficult times.

5. Practice Mindful Spending: Mindful spending means being intentional with your money and making conscious decisions about where you spend it. This can help you avoid impulse purchases and overspending, which can undermine your financial resilience. Before making a purchase, ask yourself if it's something you really need or if it's something that will bring you long-term value. Mindful spending can also help you identify areas where you can save money and put it towards your financial goals.

Building financial resilience is a process that takes time and effort, but it's essential for our financial well-being and peace of mind. By building an emergency fund, creating a budget, paying off debt, diversifying our income, and practicing mindful spending, we can build the financial resilience we need to face unexpected challenges and achieve our long-term financial goals. With a positive mindset and a solid plan, we can build the financial resilience we need to live a more secure and fulfilling life.

Strategies for Overcoming Financial Setbacks

In life, there are bound to be financial setbacks that can derail even the best-laid plans. However, these setbacks do not have to define your financial future. With the right mindset and strategies, you can overcome financial setbacks and emerge stronger and more financially resilient than ever before.

In this chapter, we will explore the various strategies for overcoming financial setbacks, including practical steps you can take to regain control of your finances and emotional techniques to help you stay positive and focused during difficult times.

1. Assess Your Current Financial Situation

The first step in overcoming a financial setback is to take stock of your current financial situation. This includes assessing your income, expenses, debts, and assets. By understanding your financial standing, you can identify areas where you can make changes to improve your financial situation.

Consider creating a budget to help you track your expenses and find areas where you can cut back. You may also want to explore ways to increase your income, such as taking on a side job or freelance work.

2. Create a Plan to Address Your Financial Setback

Once you have a clear understanding of your financial situation, the next step is to create a plan to address your setback. This may involve developing a debt-repayment plan, negotiating with creditors or lenders, or finding ways to reduce your expenses.

When creating your plan, it's important to set realistic goals and timelines. Consider breaking down your plan into smaller, more manageable steps to help you stay focused and motivated.

3. Seek Professional Help

If you are struggling to overcome a financial setback on your own, it may be helpful to seek professional help. Consider working with a financial advisor or counselor who can provide guidance and support as you navigate your financial challenges.

You may also want to consider joining a support group or seeking the advice of friends and family members who have experienced similar setbacks. Talking with others who have been through similar situations can help you feel less alone and provide you with valuable insights and strategies for overcoming your challenges.

4. Practice Self-Care

Financial setbacks can be emotionally draining, and it's important to take care of yourself during this time. Consider incorporating self-care practices into your daily routine, such as exercise, meditation, or journaling.

You may also want to seek the support of a therapist or counselor who can help you work through the emotions that come with financial setbacks, such as anxiety, stress, and depression.

5. Stay Positive and Focused on Your Goals

Finally, it's important to stay positive and focused on your goals as you work to overcome your financial setback. This may involve practicing positive self-talk and visualization techniques to help you stay motivated and optimistic about your future.

Remember, setbacks are temporary and do not define your financial future. By staying focused on your goals and implementing the strategies outlined in this chapter, you can overcome any financial setback and emerge stronger and more financially resilient than ever before.

Overcoming financial setbacks is a process that requires both practical and emotional strategies. By assessing your current financial situation, creating a plan, seeking professional help, practicing self-care, and staying positive and focused on your goals, you can overcome any financial challenge and emerge stronger and more financially resilient than ever before.

The Benefits of a Resilient Financial Mindset

In today's fast-paced world, financial setbacks are inevitable. Whether it's a job loss, unexpected expenses, or a market downturn, financial challenges can quickly throw off your plans and put you under immense stress. However, developing a resilient financial mindset can help you weather these setbacks and come out stronger on the other side.

A resilient financial mindset is one that allows you to navigate uncertainty and adapt to changing circumstances while still maintaining a positive outlook on your financial future. Here are some of the benefits of cultivating a resilient financial mindset.

1. Reduced stress and anxiety: One of the main benefits of a resilient financial mindset is reduced stress and anxiety. When you have confidence in your ability to navigate financial setbacks, you'll

be less likely to feel overwhelmed and anxious when unexpected events arise.

2. Increased financial well-being: A resilient financial mindset can help you achieve greater financial well-being over time. By developing the skills and attitudes necessary to weather financial challenges, you'll be better equipped to make sound financial decisions and achieve your long-term goals.

3. Improved decision-making: Financial resilience requires a high degree of self-awareness and the ability to remain calm and focused under pressure. As you develop these skills, you'll find that you're better able to make thoughtful, deliberate decisions that align with your values and goals.

4. Greater self-reliance: A resilient financial mindset also fosters greater self-reliance. When you're confident in your ability to handle financial setbacks, you're less likely to rely on others for support or to make impulsive decisions that could negatively impact your financial well-being.

Developing a resilient financial mindset is essential for achieving long-term financial well-being. By cultivating a growth mindset, building a strong financial foundation, practicing mindfulness, seeking support, and focusing on what you can control, you'll be better equipped to navigate financial challenges and emerge stronger on the other side.

The Connection Between Health and Wealth

Understanding the Link Between Health and Wealth

In today's world, many people equate success with material wealth. However, true success cannot be achieved without good health. There is a strong link between health and wealth, as they are both integral components of a fulfilling life. In this chapter, we will explore the connection between health and wealth, and the impact they have on each other.

The Relationship between Health and Wealth

Health and wealth are often interdependent. Poor health can lead to a decrease in wealth, and a lack of wealth can result in poor health. For example, if you are unwell, you may not be able to work, and as a result, your income may decrease. On the other hand, if you are not financially stable, you may not be able to afford healthcare, leading to poor health.

The Link between Mental and Physical Health

Mental health plays a vital role in overall well-being. A healthy mind can lead to a healthy body, and vice versa. Stress, anxiety, and depression can impact physical health and affect your ability to work and earn money. Additionally, physical health conditions such as chronic pain or illness can take a toll on mental health and impact your ability to focus and make sound financial decisions.

Investing in Health and Wealth

Investing in both health and wealth is crucial to living a fulfilling life. When we prioritize our health, we have the energy and focus to pursue our financial goals. By investing in our wealth, we can create financial security that can help us to manage health-related expenses and reduce stress.

Strategies for Investing in Health and Wealth

Here are some strategies for investing in your health and wealth:

1. Prioritize Your Health: Take care of your body by eating a healthy diet, getting enough sleep, and exercising regularly. Additionally, prioritize your mental health by practicing stress-reducing activities like meditation or mindfulness.
2. Set Financial Goals: Identify your financial goals and develop a plan to achieve them. Consider working with a financial advisor to help you develop a plan that aligns with your values and long-term objectives.
3. Diversify Your Investments: Diversify your investments to manage risk and protect your wealth. Consider investing in stocks, bonds, real estate, and other assets that align with your risk tolerance and financial goals.
4. Build an Emergency Fund: Establish an emergency fund to help manage unexpected expenses that may arise due to health-related issues or other unforeseen circumstances.
5. Seek Professional Advice: Work with professionals, such as a financial advisor or

healthcare provider, to make informed decisions about your health and wealth.

The Benefits of a Holistic Approach to Health and Wealth

A holistic approach to health and wealth recognizes the interconnectedness of these two important aspects of life. By investing in both our health and wealth, we can create a balanced and fulfilling life. A holistic approach also recognizes the importance of mindfulness, gratitude, and other spiritual practices that can enhance our overall well-being.

The link between health and wealth cannot be ignored. By prioritizing both our health and wealth, we can create a fulfilling life that is sustainable and resilient. It is important to remember that true success is not just about material wealth, but also about having good health and a sense of purpose.

Strategies for Cultivating a Healthy Mindset for Financial Prosperity

Wealth and health are two of the most important assets in life. While wealth may give you financial security, health provides the foundation for a fulfilling and happy life. However, the two are deeply interconnected, and a healthy mindset is critical to achieving financial prosperity. In this chapter, we will explore strategies to cultivate a healthy mindset that supports your financial goals and overall well-being.

1. Practice Gratitude: One of the most powerful tools to cultivate a healthy mindset is practicing gratitude. Gratitude helps you focus on what you have rather than what you lack, which is key to developing a positive attitude towards your finances. When you focus on gratitude, you naturally feel more content and satisfied, which helps to reduce stress and increase resilience in the face of financial challenges.

To practice gratitude, start by reflecting on the things you are grateful for in your life. This can be as simple as being grateful for a roof over your head, food on the table, or the love of family and friends. Make a habit of expressing gratitude each day, whether through journaling, prayer, or sharing your thoughts with loved ones.

2. Cultivate a Growth Mindset: A growth mindset is a belief that your abilities and intelligence can be developed through effort and hard work. This mindset is essential for financial success, as it helps you view challenges as opportunities for growth rather than setbacks. By embracing a growth mindset, you become more open to learning and new experiences, which can lead to new opportunities for wealth creation.

To cultivate a growth mindset, start by embracing challenges and viewing them as opportunities for growth. Challenge yourself to learn new skills, take on new responsibilities, and seek out new experiences that stretch your abilities. Embrace failure as a natural part of the learning process and use it as an opportunity to learn and improve.

3. Set Realistic Goals: Setting realistic financial goals is critical to cultivating a healthy mindset. Unrealistic goals can lead to frustration, disappointment, and feelings of failure, while achievable goals provide a sense of accomplishment and motivation to continue on your financial journey.

To set realistic goals, start by assessing your current financial situation and identifying areas where you would like to improve. Consider both short-term and long-term goals, such as paying off debt, saving for retirement, or investing in a new business venture. Be sure to set goals that are specific, measurable, and achievable within a given timeframe.

4. Practice Self-Care: Self-care is essential to maintaining a healthy mindset for financial prosperity. Taking care of your physical, emotional, and mental well-being helps to reduce stress and increase resilience, which is critical when facing financial challenges.

To practice self-care, make time for activities that nourish your mind, body, and spirit. This may include exercise, meditation, spending time in nature, or engaging in hobbies that bring you joy. Prioritize getting enough sleep, eating a healthy diet, and seeking support from loved ones when needed.

5. Seek Out Financial Education: Financial education is a powerful tool for cultivating a healthy mindset for financial prosperity. By learning about personal finance, investing, and wealth creation, you gain the knowledge and

skills to make informed decisions about your financial future.

To seek out financial education, start by reading books, attending workshops or seminars, or taking online courses on personal finance and investing. Consider seeking out a financial advisor or mentor who can provide guidance and support on your financial journey.

Cultivating a healthy mindset is critical to achieving financial prosperity and overall well-being. By practicing gratitude, cultivating a growth mindset, setting realistic goals, practicing self-care, and seeking out financial education, you can develop the habits and attitudes that support your financial goals and overall well-being. Remember that developing a healthy mindset is

Tips for Prioritizing Health and Wellness for Financial Success

Many people think that money and wealth are the key to happiness and success. However, what they often overlook is the importance of physical and mental health. Without a healthy body and mind, it can be difficult to achieve and maintain financial success. This chapter explores the connection between health and wealth and provides tips for prioritizing health and wellness for financial success.

The Link Between Health and Wealth:

There is a clear link between health and wealth. Studies have shown that people who prioritize their health and well-being are more likely to experience financial success. This is because a healthy body and mind can lead to increased productivity, focus, and creativity, which can translate into higher earnings and more opportunities.

On the other hand, neglecting your health can have serious financial consequences. Chronic illnesses and medical bills can quickly deplete your savings and negatively impact your ability to work and earn money. Additionally, a lack of focus, energy, and motivation can lead to missed opportunities and lower earnings potential.

Strategies for Cultivating a Healthy Mindset for Financial Prosperity:

1. Prioritize Self-Care: Self-care should be a top priority for anyone looking to achieve financial success. This includes regular exercise, healthy eating habits, and getting enough sleep. By taking care of your physical health, you will have more energy and focus to put towards your financial goals.
2. Practice Mindfulness: Mindfulness is the practice of being fully present in the moment. It can help reduce stress and anxiety, improve focus, and increase productivity. Incorporating mindfulness practices such as meditation or deep breathing into your daily routine can help you stay focused on your financial goals.
3. Set Realistic Goals: Setting realistic financial goals is important, but so is setting realistic health goals. Make sure you are not pushing yourself too hard in either area, as this can lead to burnout and frustration.

4. Find a Support System: Having a support system in place can help you stay motivated and accountable for both your health and financial goals. Consider joining a workout group or financial planning group to connect with like-minded individuals.

5. Cultivate Gratitude: Gratitude is a powerful tool for improving mental and emotional well-being. Take time each day to reflect on what you are grateful for, whether it be your health, your job, or your financial situation. This can help shift your mindset towards abundance and positivity.

Tips for Prioritizing Health and Wellness for Financial Success:

1. Make Time for Exercise: Regular exercise can help reduce stress, improve focus, and increase energy levels. Make time in your schedule for physical activity, whether it be a workout class or a daily walk.

2. Practice Healthy Eating Habits: Eating a balanced diet can help improve overall health and well-being. Incorporate plenty of fruits, vegetables, and whole grains into your meals, and limit processed and sugary foods.

3. Get Enough Sleep: Getting enough sleep is essential for physical and mental health. Aim for at least seven hours of sleep each night to help improve focus, reduce stress, and boost energy levels.

4. Practice Stress-Relieving Activities: Stress can have a negative impact on both physical and mental health. Incorporating stress-relieving activities such as yoga, meditation, or deep

breathing can help reduce stress levels and improve overall well-being.

5. Schedule Regular Check-Ups: Regular check-ups with your doctor or healthcare provider can help catch and prevent health issues before they become more serious and costly. Don't neglect your health, even when you're busy pursuing financial success.

Prioritizing health and wellness is essential for achieving and maintaining financial success. By taking care of your physical and mental health, you can improve productivity, creativity, and overall well-being, which can lead to increased earnings potential and more opportunities. Incorporate these strategies and tips into your daily

The Role of Self-Care in Financial Well-being

Understanding the Importance of Self-Care for Financial Success

When people think about financial success, they often focus on strategies such as budgeting, saving, and investing. However, there is another critical component to achieving financial success that often gets overlooked: self-care. In today's fast-paced world, it's easy to neglect self-care, but it's essential for overall well-being and financial prosperity.

Self-care involves taking care of oneself mentally, physically, and emotionally. It includes engaging in activities that bring joy, reducing stress levels, getting enough sleep, eating healthily, and exercising regularly. Self-care practices can significantly impact a person's financial success. Here are some ways self-care can help you achieve financial prosperity:

1. Better Decision Making: When people are exhausted or overwhelmed, they are more likely to make poor financial decisions. Self-care practices help people reduce stress and take care of their bodies, leading to a clearer mind and better decision-making skills.
2. Improved Physical Health: Investing in your physical health can reduce the likelihood of developing chronic conditions such as diabetes or high blood pressure, which can lead to high medical bills and lost income.

3. Reduced Stress: Financial stress is a significant contributor to poor mental and physical health. Engaging in self-care activities such as meditation, yoga, or massage can reduce stress levels and help individuals maintain a positive attitude towards their financial goals.
4. Increased Productivity: When people are taking care of themselves, they are more likely to be productive, focused, and engaged in their work. This can lead to better job performance, career advancement, and increased earning potential.
5. Enhanced Creativity: Self-care practices can stimulate creativity, leading to innovative financial strategies that can enhance one's financial success.

Tips for Practicing Self-Care for Financial Success:

1. Prioritize Sleep: Getting enough sleep is essential for overall well-being and can significantly impact one's financial success. Establish a regular sleep routine and aim to get 7-9 hours of sleep per night.
2. Exercise Regularly: Exercise is a great way to reduce stress, improve physical health, and enhance cognitive function. Incorporate regular physical activity into your daily routine, such as going for a walk or doing yoga.
3. Eat Healthily: A balanced and nutritious diet can improve physical health and provide the energy needed to achieve financial success. Prioritize eating whole foods, such as fruits, vegetables, and lean protein.
4. Practice Mindfulness: Mindfulness practices such as meditation and deep breathing can help reduce

stress levels, improve mental clarity, and enhance decision-making skills.

5. Take Breaks: Regular breaks throughout the day can reduce stress and enhance productivity. Take a few minutes every hour to stretch, walk around, or engage in a self-care activity.
6. Engage in Joyful Activities: Taking time for activities that bring joy and relaxation can reduce stress levels and improve overall well-being. Consider engaging in activities such as reading, listening to music, or spending time with loved ones.

Self-care is essential for achieving financial success. By prioritizing self-care practices such as getting enough sleep, exercising regularly, eating healthily, and engaging in mindfulness practices, individuals can enhance their decision-making skills, reduce stress levels, increase productivity, and achieve their financial goals. By taking care of oneself mentally, physically, and emotionally, one can create a solid foundation for financial prosperity.

How to Incorporate Self-Care into Your Money Habits

Money management can often feel overwhelming and stressful. However, incorporating self-care practices into your money habits can help alleviate these feelings and promote a healthy financial mindset. In this chapter, we will discuss how to incorporate self-care into your money habits.

Self-care is the practice of taking care of your physical, emotional, and mental health. It involves prioritizing your well-being and making intentional choices to nurture yourself. When it comes to money management, self-care can be a powerful tool to reduce financial stress and increase financial success.

One way to incorporate self-care into your money habits is to create a budget that prioritizes self-care expenses. This can include things like gym memberships, therapy sessions, healthy food choices, or any other activities that support your well-being. By prioritizing these expenses in your budget, you are sending a message to yourself that self-care is important and should not be sacrificed for financial gain.

Another way to incorporate self-care into your money habits is to set financial boundaries. This means learning to say no to expenses that do not align with your values or goals, even if they may be tempting in the moment. For example, if you have set a goal to pay off your credit card debt, saying no to a shopping spree with friends can be a form of self-care, as it aligns with your financial goals and promotes long-term financial health.

In addition to setting financial boundaries, it is important to regularly check in with yourself and evaluate your financial habits. This can include reviewing your budget, tracking your expenses, and assessing any emotional or mental barriers that may be impacting your relationship with money. By taking the time to reflect on your financial habits and emotional well-being, you can identify areas for improvement and create a more sustainable and healthy financial mindset.

Finally, incorporating self-care into your money habits also involves celebrating your financial successes.

Whether it's paying off a credit card, saving for a down payment on a home, or achieving any other financial goal, taking the time to acknowledge and celebrate your accomplishments can be a form of self-care. It not only boosts your confidence and motivation but also reminds you of the importance of prioritizing your financial health.

Incorporating self-care into your money habits may feel challenging at first, especially if you are used to prioritizing financial gain over your well-being. However, by making intentional choices to prioritize self-care, you can create a more sustainable and healthy financial mindset that promotes long-term financial success.

The Benefits of Prioritizing Self-Care for Your Finances

In our society, we often associate financial success with hard work, dedication, and a laser focus on making money. However, the truth is that success in any area of life requires a balance of physical, mental, and emotional well-being. In fact, prioritizing self-care can have a profound impact on our financial success, as it allows us to approach money from a place of abundance, clarity, and calm.

One of the main benefits of prioritizing self-care for your finances is that it helps you to maintain a healthy relationship with money. When we neglect our physical and emotional well-being in the pursuit of wealth, it's easy to become consumed by money-related stress, anxiety, and worry. This can lead to a scarcity mindset, where we believe that there's never enough money to go around and that we must constantly be chasing after more. However, when we make self-care a priority, we shift our focus away from external factors and begin to cultivate a sense of internal abundance. We start to see money as a tool for creating a fulfilling life, rather than the end goal in itself.

In addition to helping us maintain a healthy relationship with money, self-care can also have a positive impact on our earning potential. When we prioritize our physical and emotional well-being, we're better equipped to handle the challenges and stresses that come with building wealth. We have more energy, focus, and creativity, which can help us to innovate, take risks, and pursue new opportunities. We're also more likely to make smart financial decisions, as we're able to approach money from a place of clarity and calm rather than fear and panic.

Another benefit of prioritizing self-care for your finances is that it helps you to stay motivated and focused on your long-term financial goals. When we neglect our physical and emotional well-being, it's easy to become overwhelmed by the demands of everyday life and lose sight of our larger vision for our finances. However, when we make self-care a priority, we create a foundation of stability and support that allows us to stay committed to our goals over the long term. We're able to approach our finances with a sense of purpose and intention, knowing that we're taking care of ourselves in the process.

So, how can you start prioritizing self-care for your finances? The first step is to make a conscious effort to take care of your physical and emotional well-being on a regular basis. This may mean carving out time in your schedule for exercise, meditation, or other stress-reducing activities. It may also mean seeking out professional support, such as therapy or financial counseling, to help you navigate the challenges of building wealth. Additionally, it's important to cultivate a sense of gratitude and abundance in your daily life, focusing on the positive aspects of your financial situation rather than dwelling on the negative.

Prioritizing self-care is essential for achieving financial success and creating a fulfilling life. By taking care of our physical and emotional well-being, we're able to approach money from a place of abundance, clarity, and calm, which can help us to make smart financial decisions and stay motivated and focused on our long-term goals. So, make self-care a priority in your life and watch as your financial prosperity grows in abundance.

The Power of Forgiveness in Financial Healing

The Connection Between Forgiveness and Financial Healing

Money-related stress and anxiety can cause significant emotional pain and lead to physical health problems. Financial difficulties can strain relationships, create feelings of shame and guilt, and negatively affect one's self-esteem. However, one way to alleviate the burden of financial stress is through forgiveness. Forgiveness is a powerful tool that can bring financial healing and freedom.

Forgiveness is often associated with relationships, but it can also be applied to finances. Forgiveness is the process of releasing negative emotions and letting go of grudges, resentments, and grievances. It involves acknowledging the pain caused by a financial situation and choosing to let go of it. Forgiveness is not about forgetting what happened or condoning unacceptable behavior. Instead, it is a conscious decision to release the negative emotions that are associated with the situation.

Forgiveness is an act of self-care. Holding on to anger, bitterness, and resentment can lead to stress and anxiety. When we forgive, we release those negative emotions, and in turn, we free ourselves from their damaging effects. Forgiveness can also improve relationships and help us move forward from a financial setback.

Studies have shown that practicing forgiveness can lead to physical and emotional benefits, including reduced stress and anxiety, improved mental health, and lower blood pressure. When we forgive, we release the stress associated with the situation, which can improve our overall well-being.

Forgiveness is also essential for financial healing. It allows us to let go of the past and move forward towards financial freedom. When we hold on to resentment and anger, we may feel stuck in our financial situation. Forgiveness allows us to release those negative emotions and open ourselves up to new opportunities and possibilities. Forgiveness is also important for developing a healthy relationship with money. When we forgive ourselves for past financial mistakes, we can move forward with a more positive and empowered mindset.

Forgiveness is not always easy, and it may take time to process and release negative emotions. However, there are strategies that can help facilitate the forgiveness process. One strategy is to practice empathy towards the person or situation that caused the financial pain. Empathy involves putting ourselves in another's shoes and understanding their perspective. Another strategy is to focus on the positive aspects of the situation and look for opportunities for growth and learning.

Forgiveness is a powerful tool that can bring financial healing and freedom. It allows us to release negative emotions, reduce stress and anxiety, and improve our overall well-being. Forgiveness is also essential for developing a healthy relationship with money and moving forward towards financial freedom. While forgiveness may not be easy, practicing empathy and focusing on the positive aspects of a situation can help facilitate the forgiveness process.

Strategies for Forgiving Yourself and Others for Financial Mistakes

One of the first steps in forgiving yourself and others for financial mistakes is to acknowledge the pain and frustration that may have been caused. It can be helpful to reflect on the situation and identify any lessons that can be learned from it, without blaming or shaming yourself or others. This can allow for a sense of understanding and compassion, which is the foundation for forgiveness.

Another strategy for forgiving financial mistakes is to practice self-compassion. It can be easy to be hard on ourselves when we make financial errors, but treating ourselves with kindness and understanding can help to release the negative emotions associated with these mistakes. This might involve giving ourselves permission to make mistakes and recognizing that they do not define our worth as individuals.

It is also important to recognize the power of forgiveness in our relationships with others. When we hold onto anger or resentment towards others who may have caused us financial harm, it can be difficult to move forward and create positive relationships. By practicing forgiveness towards others, we can release ourselves from the negative emotions associated with past hurts and create a sense of peace and understanding in our relationships.

A spiritual perspective on forgiveness can also be helpful in cultivating a mindset of forgiveness. Many spiritual traditions emphasize the importance of forgiveness as a means of releasing negative energy and promoting healing. By connecting with a higher power and seeking guidance in the process of forgiveness, we can cultivate a sense of inner peace and trust in the journey towards financial healing.

Overall, forgiveness is a powerful tool for financial healing and prosperity. By acknowledging past mistakes and treating ourselves and others with compassion and understanding, we can release negative emotions and create space for positive financial experiences.

The Benefits of Letting Go of Resentment for Financial Abundance

The way we think and feel about money can significantly impact our financial well-being. One of the most common emotions associated with money is resentment, which can be directed towards ourselves or others for past financial mistakes. However, holding onto this resentment can limit our ability to attract abundance and financial prosperity. In this chapter, we will explore the benefits of letting go of resentment and strategies for cultivating forgiveness in our financial lives.

The Benefits of Letting Go of Resentment: When we hold onto resentment towards ourselves or others for financial mistakes, we create negative energy that can block the flow of abundance into our lives. This negative energy can manifest as feelings of scarcity, fear, and anxiety, making it difficult to attract opportunities for financial growth and success.

On the other hand, when we cultivate forgiveness and let go of resentment, we create a positive energy that attracts abundance and prosperity. Forgiveness can help us release negative emotions and limiting beliefs that may be holding us back from achieving our financial goals. It can also increase our self-esteem and sense of worthiness, allowing us to believe that we deserve financial abundance.

Strategies for Cultivating Forgiveness in Your Financial Life:

1. Practice self-compassion: Start by being kind and compassionate towards yourself for any past financial mistakes. Recognize that everyone makes mistakes and that it's a part of the learning process. Instead of dwelling on past mistakes, focus on what you can do differently in the future.

2. Reframe your perspective: Try to see past financial mistakes as opportunities for growth and learning. Instead of seeing them as failures, view them as lessons that can help you make better financial decisions in the future.

3. Focus on gratitude: Gratitude is a powerful tool for cultivating forgiveness and releasing resentment. Take time each day to focus on the things you're grateful for, including your financial blessings. By focusing on what you have, you'll be less likely to hold onto negative feelings about what you don't have.

4. Practice forgiveness meditation: Forgiveness meditation is a technique that involves visualizing the person or situation you need to forgive and sending them love and compassion. This practice

can help release negative emotions and promote feelings of forgiveness and compassion.

5. Seek support: If you're struggling to let go of resentment towards yourself or others, consider seeking support from a therapist or financial coach. They can help you work through your emotions and develop strategies for cultivating forgiveness in your financial life.

Letting go of resentment and cultivating forgiveness can be a powerful tool for attracting financial abundance and prosperity. By releasing negative emotions and limiting beliefs, we create space for positive energy and opportunities to flow into our lives. With practice and patience, anyone can cultivate forgiveness and experience the benefits of a more abundant financial life.

The Importance of Taking Action Towards Financial Goals

The Connection Between Action and Financial Success

Many people dream of achieving financial success but only a few truly succeed. The reason for this is not always because they lack knowledge or resources, but rather because they lack the right mindset and attitude towards taking action. In this chapter, we will explore the connection between action and financial success, and how you can cultivate the mindset necessary to take action towards your financial goals.

The Importance of Taking Action: Taking action is an essential component of achieving financial success. Without action, dreams and plans remain only ideas without any manifestation. By taking action, we are able to turn our ideas into reality and make our financial dreams a possibility. It is important to note that taking action does not mean reckless or impulsive decision making. It is about taking calculated and strategic steps towards achieving your goals.

Cultivating a Mindset for Action: The first step towards taking action is cultivating the right mindset. A mindset that is positive, determined, and focused on growth. This mindset requires a willingness to take risks, learn from mistakes, and continuously improve.

The Benefits of Taking Action: Taking action towards your financial goals has numerous benefits. These include:

1. Increased confidence: When you take action and see progress, you gain confidence in your abilities and your vision.
2. Expanded opportunities: By taking action, you open yourself up to new opportunities that you may not have considered before.
3. Improved decision-making skills: Taking action requires making decisions, and with practice, you will develop better decision-making skills.
4. Reduced stress: Procrastination and inaction can lead to stress and anxiety. By taking action, you reduce stress and create a sense of control over your financial situation.

Taking action is an essential component of achieving financial success. It requires a mindset that is focused on growth, willingness to take risks, and the ability to learn from mistakes. By cultivating a mindset for action, setting specific goals, and taking consistent steps towards achieving them, you can increase your confidence, expand opportunities, improve decision-making skills, and reduce stress. Remember that financial success is within your reach if you are willing to take action towards achieving it.

How to Overcome Procrastination and Take Action Towards Your Financial Goals

Procrastination can be a major obstacle in achieving financial success. When we put off important tasks related to our finances, we may miss out on opportunities to grow our wealth and achieve our financial goals. Overcoming procrastination requires a combination of mindfulness, self-awareness, and a willingness to take action. In this chapter, we will explore some strategies for overcoming procrastination and taking action towards your financial goals.

1. Practice mindfulness: Mindfulness is a powerful tool for overcoming procrastination. By being fully present in the moment, we can become more aware of our thoughts and feelings and the reasons why we may be procrastinating. When we are mindful, we can better understand our motivations and make conscious choices about how to move forward. You can practice mindfulness through meditation, yoga, or simply by taking a few deep breaths and focusing on the present moment.

2. Set realistic goals: One of the reasons why we may procrastinate is because we feel overwhelmed by the size or complexity of the task at hand. To overcome this, it's important to break your financial goals down into smaller, more manageable steps. By setting realistic goals that you can achieve in the short-term, you can build momentum and gain confidence in your ability to take action.

3. Create a plan of action: Having a clear plan of action can help you overcome procrastination and take action towards your financial goals. Write down the specific steps you need to take to achieve your goals and assign deadlines for each step. This will help you stay focused and motivated, and ensure that you are making progress towards your financial goals.

4. Hold yourself accountable: Accountability is key to overcoming procrastination. You can hold yourself accountable by setting up regular check-

ins with yourself or with a trusted friend or advisor. Use these check-ins to review your progress, celebrate your successes, and identify areas where you may need to make adjustments.

5. Focus on the benefits of taking action: Finally, it's important to focus on the benefits of taking action towards your financial goals. By reminding yourself of the positive outcomes that will come from taking action, you can stay motivated and overcome the temptation to procrastinate. Whether it's the satisfaction of achieving your goals, the financial freedom that comes with increased wealth, or the peace of mind that comes from being in control of your finances, there are many reasons to take action towards your financial goals.

Overcoming procrastination requires a combination of mindfulness, self-awareness, and a willingness to take action. By setting realistic goals, creating a plan of action, holding yourself accountable, and focusing on the benefits of taking action, you can overcome procrastination and achieve your financial goals. Remember, the most important step is always the first one, so take that step today towards your financial success.

Tips for Staying Motivated in Pursuit of Financial Prosperity

Motivation is a key component of achieving any goal, including financial success. However, staying motivated can be challenging, especially when faced with setbacks or obstacles. In this chapter, we will explore tips and strategies for staying motivated in pursuit of financial prosperity.

1. Set Clear Goals

One of the most important ways to stay motivated is to set clear and specific goals. When you have a clear idea of what you want to achieve, you can focus your energy and efforts towards that goal. Your financial goals should be realistic, measurable, and have a clear timeline.

For example, rather than saying, "I want to save money," you can set a specific goal such as, "I want to save $5,000 for a down payment on a new home within the next 12 months."

2. Break Goals Down into Smaller Steps

Breaking down your larger financial goals into smaller, achievable steps can help you stay motivated. This approach can make the goal seem less daunting and allow you to track your progress.

For example, if your goal is to pay off a credit card debt of $10,000, you can break it down into smaller steps such as paying off $1,000 per month for 10 months.

3. Visualize Success

Visualization is a powerful tool that can help you stay motivated in pursuit of financial prosperity. Visualize yourself achieving your financial goals, and imagine how it will feel to have financial freedom and security. You can also create a vision board with pictures and quotes that represent your financial goals and aspirations.

4. Stay Positive and Grateful

Maintaining a positive mindset and gratitude can help you stay motivated in challenging times. When faced with setbacks or obstacles, try to reframe your mindset and focus on the positive. Take time to acknowledge what you have achieved so far, and be grateful for the progress you have made.

5. Find an Accountability Partner

Having an accountability partner can help you stay motivated and on track towards your financial goals. This could be a friend, family member, or a professional such as a financial advisor or coach. Share your goals with your accountability partner and set up regular check-ins to track progress and offer support.

6. Celebrate Small Wins

Celebrating small wins along the way can help you stay motivated and maintain momentum towards your larger financial goals. When you achieve a smaller milestone, such as paying off a credit card or saving a certain amount of money, take time to acknowledge and celebrate your progress.

7. Learn from Setbacks

Finally, it is important to learn from setbacks and mistakes along the way. Financial setbacks are a natural part of the journey towards financial prosperity. Instead of getting discouraged, use setbacks as an opportunity to learn, adjust, and grow.

Staying motivated in pursuit of financial prosperity is not always easy, but with these tips and strategies, you can stay focused and on track towards your goals. Remember to stay positive, celebrate small wins, and learn from setbacks. With persistence and determination, you can achieve financial success and abundance.

The Connection Between Mindset and Financial Freedom

Understanding the Link Between Mindset and Financial Freedom

Achieving financial freedom is a common goal for many people, and while it may seem like a lofty aspiration, it is entirely possible. The key to achieving financial freedom lies in the mindset you cultivate around money. This chapter will explore the link between mindset and financial freedom, and provide you with valuable insights and strategies to help you achieve this goal.

Your mindset plays a critical role in your relationship with money. If you have a scarcity mindset, you may constantly worry about not having enough money, and may feel like you are always struggling to make ends meet. On the other hand, if you have an abundance mindset, you believe that there is enough money to go around and that you can create as much wealth as you desire.

One of the most significant benefits of cultivating a mindset of abundance is that it allows you to see opportunities that you may have otherwise missed. When you focus on scarcity, you are more likely to see limitations and obstacles. However, when you adopt an abundance mindset, you begin to see possibilities and opportunities that were previously hidden from view.

Another benefit of having a positive financial mindset is that it allows you to be more resilient in the face of financial challenges. When you have an abundance mindset, you believe that you can overcome obstacles and that setbacks are temporary. This resilience allows you to bounce back quickly when things don't go as planned.

One of the most significant obstacles to achieving financial freedom is debt. If you are constantly worrying about debt and struggling to make payments, it can be challenging to see a way out. However, with the right mindset, you can overcome this obstacle and achieve financial freedom.

To cultivate a mindset of financial freedom, you must first acknowledge that your thoughts and beliefs around money are not set in stone. You have the power to change them, and by doing so, you can change your financial situation.

One way to change your mindset is by changing the way you talk to yourself about money. If you find yourself constantly saying things like, "I'll never be able to get out of debt," or "I'll never be able to save enough for retirement," you are reinforcing a negative mindset. Instead, try to focus on positive statements like, "I am taking steps to pay off my debt," or "I am making progress towards my financial goals."

Another way to cultivate a mindset of financial freedom is by surrounding yourself with positive influences. Seek out mentors and friends who have achieved financial success, and learn from their experiences. Read books and attend seminars that focus on personal finance and wealth-building. By surrounding yourself with positivity, you can begin to shift your mindset towards abundance.

Finally, taking action towards your financial goals is an essential part of cultivating a mindset of financial freedom. It is not enough to simply wish for financial abundance; you must take concrete steps towards achieving it. Create a budget, pay off debt, and start investing in your future. By taking action, you will begin to see progress towards your goals, which will reinforce your positive mindset.

The link between mindset and financial freedom is clear. By cultivating a mindset of abundance and taking positive action towards your financial goals, you can achieve financial freedom and live the life you have always dreamed of. Remember that your thoughts and beliefs around money are not set in stone; you have the power to change them and create the financial future you desire.

Strategies for Cultivating a Prosperous Mindset for Financial Independence

Financial independence is a goal that many people aspire to achieve. It is the state of having enough money and resources to live the life you desire, without relying on someone else's support. However, financial independence is not just about accumulating wealth, it is also about having the right mindset. A prosperous mindset is essential for financial independence as it helps you make better financial decisions, stay motivated, and overcome challenges. In this chapter, we will discuss some effective strategies for cultivating a prosperous mindset for financial independence.

1. Develop a Positive Attitude towards Money

Your attitude towards money plays a significant role in your financial success. If you have negative beliefs about money, you may struggle to accumulate wealth. To cultivate a prosperous mindset, you need to develop a positive attitude towards money. Start by acknowledging that money is a valuable tool that can help you achieve your goals and live a fulfilling life. Focus on the opportunities and abundance that money can bring into your life, rather than on the limitations and scarcity.

2. Set Clear Financial Goals

Setting clear financial goals is essential for achieving financial independence. It helps you stay focused and motivated, and makes it easier to track your progress. To set effective financial goals, you need to be specific, measurable, and realistic. Break down your long-term financial goals into smaller, achievable milestones, and celebrate your progress along the way. This will help you stay motivated and maintain a positive outlook.

3. Practice Gratitude

Gratitude is an essential component of a prosperous mindset. When you focus on what you are grateful for, you attract more positive experiences into your life. Make a habit of expressing gratitude for the blessings in your life, including your financial resources. Even if you are currently facing financial challenges, try to focus on the positive aspects of your situation, such as the lessons you are learning or the people who are supporting you.

4. Cultivate a Growth Mindset

A growth mindset is the belief that your abilities and intelligence can be developed through hard work and dedication. Cultivating a growth mindset is essential for achieving financial independence as it helps you stay motivated and overcome obstacles. Embrace challenges and see them as opportunities to learn and grow. Instead of focusing on your failures or limitations, focus on your strengths and potential.

5. Take Calculated Risks

Taking calculated risks is a crucial component of achieving financial independence. However, it is important to approach risk-taking with caution and make informed decisions. Before making any significant financial decisions, do your research, and seek advice from trusted sources. Be willing to take risks, but also be prepared to learn from your mistakes.

6. Practice Patience and Persistence

Financial independence is not achieved overnight; it requires patience and persistence. It is essential to stay committed to your goals, even when progress is slow or setbacks occur. Remember that every small step you take towards your goals brings you closer to financial independence. Stay patient, persistent, and trust the process.

Cultivating a prosperous mindset is essential for achieving financial independence. By developing a positive attitude towards money, setting clear financial goals, practicing gratitude, cultivating a growth mindset, taking calculated risks, and practicing patience and persistence, you can cultivate a mindset that supports your financial success. With the right mindset and actions, you can achieve financial independence and live the life you desire.

Tips for Achieving Financial Freedom

Financial freedom is a state of being where you no longer have to worry about money. It means that you have enough resources to live the life you want without being dependent on a job or other means of income. Achieving financial freedom is a goal that many people have, but few know how to attain it. In this chapter, we will discuss some tips for achieving financial freedom and how you can cultivate a mindset that supports your goal.

1. Set Clear Financial Goals: The first step towards achieving financial freedom is to set clear goals. You need to have a plan that outlines what you want to achieve and how you will get there. Start by identifying your long-term financial goals, such as retiring early or purchasing a second home. Then, break those goals down into smaller, more achievable steps, and create a timeline for each one.

2. Create a Budget: One of the most important aspects of achieving financial freedom is living within your means. Creating a budget is an effective way to track your spending and identify areas where you can cut back. By living below your means and putting money towards your

financial goals, you can start building wealth over time.

3. Pay off Debt: Debt can be a significant barrier to achieving financial freedom. It's essential to pay off high-interest debt as quickly as possible, as it can accumulate and hinder your ability to save and invest. Start by paying off your credit card debt, then move on to other types of debt, such as student loans or car loans.

4. Save and Invest: Saving and investing are crucial components of achieving financial freedom. You should aim to save at least 20% of your income and invest it in a diversified portfolio that matches your risk tolerance. By investing in stocks, bonds, and other assets, you can grow your wealth over time and create a passive income stream.

5. Maintain a Healthy Credit Score: Your credit score plays a significant role in your ability to achieve financial freedom. A good credit score can help you qualify for lower interest rates on loans and credit cards, which can save you thousands of dollars over time. You can maintain a healthy credit score by paying your bills on time, keeping your credit utilization low, and monitoring your credit report regularly.

6. Be Patient: Achieving financial freedom takes time and requires patience. It's essential to remember that you won't become financially free overnight, but rather through consistent and persistent efforts over time. Don't get discouraged if progress seems slow; instead, focus on the small wins and celebrate each milestone along the way.

7. Surround Yourself with Like-Minded People: Surrounding yourself with people who share your financial goals and values can be an effective way

to stay motivated and accountable. Joining a financial group or attending financial workshops can provide you with the support you need to achieve financial freedom.

Achieving financial freedom requires discipline, patience, and a willingness to learn and grow. By setting clear financial goals, creating a budget, paying off debt, saving and investing, maintaining a healthy credit score, being patient, and surrounding yourself with like-minded people, you can attain the financial freedom you desire. Remember that financial freedom is not just about money; it's about the freedom to live the life you want and pursue your passions without being constrained by financial worries.

The Role of Spirituality in Financial Success

The Connection Between Spirituality and Financial Well-being

The relationship between spirituality and financial well-being has been a topic of interest for many years. Some believe that spiritual practices can enhance financial success, while others argue that the two are completely unrelated. However, recent research has suggested that there is a strong link between spirituality and financial well-being.

At its core, spirituality refers to a sense of connectedness to something greater than oneself. This can take many forms, including religious practices, meditation, or simply a belief in the interconnectedness of all things. When it comes to financial well-being, spirituality can play an important role in helping individuals to create a sense of purpose and meaning in their financial lives.

One way that spirituality can contribute to financial well-being is by providing a framework for decision-making. For example, individuals who prioritize their spiritual beliefs may be more likely to make financial decisions that align with their values and beliefs. This can help to create a sense of coherence and purpose in one's financial life, which can ultimately lead to greater satisfaction and fulfillment.

Spirituality can also play a role in managing financial stress. Financial stress is a common experience for many people, and it can have negative impacts on both physical and mental health. However, individuals who have a strong spiritual practice may be better equipped to handle financial stress and maintain a sense of calm and balance in the face of financial challenges.

In addition to these benefits, spirituality can also provide a sense of abundance and gratitude, which can help individuals to cultivate a positive mindset around money. By focusing on the abundance that exists in one's life, rather than the scarcity, individuals can create a sense of optimism and hopefulness about their financial future.

So, what can you do to incorporate spirituality into your financial life? One approach is to start by identifying your core values and beliefs. What is most important to you in life? What are your priorities and goals? By understanding your values and beliefs, you can begin to make financial decisions that align with your spiritual practice.

Another approach is to incorporate spiritual practices into your financial routine. For example, you may choose to start each day with a gratitude practice, or to meditate on your financial goals and aspirations. By incorporating these practices into your daily routine, you can create a sense of mindfulness and intentionality around your finances.

Ultimately, the connection between spirituality and financial well-being is complex and multifaceted. However, by cultivating a sense of connectedness to something greater than oneself, individuals can create a sense of purpose and meaning in their financial lives, which can ultimately lead to greater satisfaction, fulfillment, and abundance.

Strategies for Cultivating a Spiritual Mindset for Financial Prosperity

Spirituality and financial prosperity may seem like an unlikely combination, but the truth is that they are deeply intertwined. Our spiritual beliefs and practices can have a significant impact on our financial well-being, as they shape our attitudes towards money and wealth. In this chapter, we will explore the strategies for cultivating a spiritual mindset for financial prosperity.

1. Practice Gratitude

Gratitude is one of the foundational principles of many spiritual traditions. When we cultivate a mindset of gratitude, we begin to see our financial situation in a different light. Instead of focusing on what we lack, we begin to appreciate what we have. This can help us make wiser financial decisions, as we become more mindful of our spending and savings habits.

To cultivate gratitude in your financial life, try keeping a gratitude journal where you write down things you are thankful for in regards to your finances. You can also practice gratitude by saying a prayer or mantra of thanks each time you pay your bills or make a financial transaction.

2. Practice Generosity

Another spiritual principle that can impact our finances is generosity. When we give to others, we tap into a sense of abundance and recognize that we have more than enough. This can help us let go of any feelings of lack or scarcity that may be holding us back financially.

To cultivate generosity in your financial life, consider making a regular donation to a charity or cause you believe in. You can also look for ways to give back to your community, such as volunteering your time or resources.

3. Practice Mindful Spending

Mindfulness is the practice of being fully present and aware in the current moment. When we bring mindfulness to our financial decisions, we can make more intentional choices that align with our values and priorities. Mindful spending involves being aware of our spending habits, tracking our expenses, and making conscious decisions about how we use our money.

To practice mindful spending, create a budget and track your expenses regularly. Before making a purchase, ask yourself if it aligns with your values and priorities. Consider whether there are alternative options that may better serve your needs and goals.

4. Cultivate Trust

Trust is another important spiritual principle that can impact our financial well-being. When we trust in the universe, a higher power, or our own intuition, we can let go of fear and anxiety around money. This can help us make more confident and empowered financial decisions.

To cultivate trust in your financial life, practice letting go of attachment to specific outcomes. Instead, focus on taking positive action towards your goals and trusting that the universe will provide what you need. You can also cultivate trust by developing a sense of inner peace through practices like meditation or prayer.

5. Connect with Like-Minded People

Finally, connecting with like-minded people can help us cultivate a spiritual mindset for financial prosperity. When we surround ourselves with people who share our values and beliefs, we can receive support and encouragement to pursue our financial goals.

To connect with like-minded people, consider joining a spiritual community or group that focuses on financial prosperity. You can also seek out networking events or online forums that align with your values and interests.

By incorporating spiritual practices into our financial lives, we can cultivate a mindset of abundance and prosperity. By practicing gratitude, generosity, mindfulness, trust, and connecting with like-minded people, we can create a more fulfilling and prosperous financial future.

Tips for Incorporating Spirituality into Your Money Habits

Many people believe that money and spirituality are incompatible. However, the truth is that spirituality can play an important role in your financial journey. When you approach money with a spiritual mindset, you can cultivate a sense of abundance and gratitude that can lead to financial prosperity. Here are some tips for incorporating spirituality into your money habits:

Set intentions

Setting intentions is a powerful way to align your financial goals with your spiritual values. Take some time to reflect on what you want to achieve financially and why it's important to you. Then, set clear intentions for what you want to create in your financial life. This will help you to stay focused and motivated as you work towards your goals.

Connect with a higher power

For many people, spirituality is about connecting with a higher power. Whether you believe in God, the universe, or some other divine force, take some time each day to connect with this power. You might do this through prayer, meditation, or simply spending time in nature. Connecting with a higher power can help you to feel more grounded and centered, and can provide a sense of perspective on your financial journey.

Practice mindfulness

Mindfulness is the practice of being fully present in the moment, without judgment. When you practice mindfulness in your financial life, you become more aware of your thoughts and feelings around money. This awareness can help you to identify any negative patterns or limiting beliefs that may be holding you back financially. By practicing mindfulness, you can learn to release these patterns and create a more positive and abundant mindset.

Give back

Finally, giving back is an important part of any spiritual practice. When you give to others, you open yourself up to receiving more abundance in your own life. Look for ways to give back to your community, whether through volunteering, donating to charity, or simply being kind to others. By giving back, you'll create a sense of connection and purpose that can help you to feel more fulfilled in your financial life.

Incorporating spirituality into your money habits is a powerful way to cultivate abundance and prosperity in your life. By practicing gratitude, setting intentions, connecting with a higher power, practicing mindfulness, and giving back, you can create a more spiritually aligned and prosperous financial life. Remember, your spirituality and your finances are not mutually exclusive - in fact, they can work together to create a more fulfilling and abundant life.

The Connection Between Mindset and Generational Wealth

Understanding the Importance of Mindset in Building Generational Wealth

When it comes to building generational wealth, mindset plays a crucial role. It is often said that wealth creation begins with a mindset shift. A person with a positive and abundant mindset is more likely to take action towards building wealth and creating a legacy that can be passed on to future generations. In this chapter, we will explore the importance of mindset in building generational wealth, and how it can impact not only our own financial success but also that of our children and grandchildren.

The Power of Mindset:

Our mindset is our mental attitude or disposition towards something. It is a set of beliefs and attitudes that shape our thoughts, behaviors, and actions. A positive mindset can help us achieve our goals, overcome obstacles, and navigate challenges with resilience. Similarly, a negative mindset can hold us back, create limiting beliefs, and prevent us from reaching our full potential.

When it comes to building generational wealth, mindset can make all the difference. Those with a positive mindset are more likely to take calculated risks, invest in assets that appreciate in value, and maintain a long-term perspective when it comes to financial planning. They are also more likely to seek out education and resources to improve their financial literacy and seek the guidance of financial advisors to create a plan that will help them achieve their financial goals.

On the other hand, those with a negative mindset may feel trapped by their financial circumstances and see themselves as victims of their circumstances. They may avoid taking risks, resist investing in their future, and lack the discipline to save and budget effectively. Without a positive mindset, it can be difficult to build generational wealth.

How Mindset Impacts Generational Wealth:

Mindset can have a significant impact on our ability to build generational wealth. When we have a positive and abundant mindset, we are more likely to take actions that lead to financial success. For example, we may seek out opportunities to learn about investing, network with successful entrepreneurs, and invest in assets that appreciate in value. We are also more likely to pass these values and behaviors down to future generations, creating a legacy of financial prosperity.

Conversely, a negative mindset can hold us back from achieving financial success and prevent us from creating generational wealth. For example, if we believe that we will never be able to achieve financial success, we may not take the steps necessary to create it. We may also pass down limiting beliefs and negative financial habits to our children and grandchildren, perpetuating a cycle of financial struggle.

Strategies for Cultivating a Positive Mindset:

If you want to build generational wealth, cultivating a positive and abundant mindset is essential. Here are some strategies that can help you develop a positive mindset:

1. Practice Gratitude: Gratitude is the foundation of abundance. When we focus on what we have, rather than what we lack, we cultivate a sense of abundance that can attract more positivity into our lives.
2. Visualize Success: Visualization is a powerful tool for achieving success. Take time to imagine what it would feel like to achieve your financial goals and create a legacy of wealth for future generations.
3. Surround Yourself with Positive Influences: Surround yourself with people who have a positive and abundant mindset. Seek out mentors and advisors who can guide you towards financial success.
4. Learn from Failure: Failure is an inevitable part of the journey towards financial success. Learn from your mistakes, and use them as an opportunity to grow and improve.
5. Practice Self-Care: Taking care of your physical, mental, and emotional well-being is essential for cultivating a positive mindset. Make time for activities that bring you joy and peace, and prioritize your health and wellness.

Building generational wealth requires more than just financial knowledge and resources. It requires a positive and abundant mindset that can overcome obstacles, take risks, and create a legacy

Strategies for Cultivating a Prosperous Mindset for Building Generational Wealth

Building generational wealth is an admirable goal that requires a mindset that goes beyond personal gain. It is a legacy that can be passed on to future generations, providing them with financial stability and opportunities. A prosperous mindset is the foundation for building generational wealth, and it requires discipline, focus, and intentionality. In this chapter, we will explore some strategies for cultivating a prosperous mindset that can help you build generational wealth.

1. Develop a Long-Term Perspective

One of the most important strategies for cultivating a prosperous mindset is to develop a long-term perspective. Building generational wealth is not an overnight process, and it requires a sustained effort over many years. It is important to have a clear vision of what you want to achieve and to focus on the steps you need to take to get there. This requires discipline and patience, as well as a willingness to delay gratification in the short term for long-term gain.

2. Embrace a Growth Mindset

A growth mindset is essential for building generational wealth. It is a mindset that sees challenges as opportunities for growth and development, rather than obstacles to be avoided. A growth mindset embraces learning and sees failure as a natural part of the learning process. By embracing a growth mindset, you can develop the skills and knowledge necessary to build wealth over the long term.

3. Cultivate a Culture of Financial Responsibility

Building generational wealth requires a culture of financial responsibility. This means developing good money habits and modeling them for your children and grandchildren. It means setting financial goals and developing a plan to achieve them. It means living within your means, avoiding debt, and saving for the future. By cultivating a culture of financial responsibility, you can set the stage for generational wealth that can be passed on for many years to come.

4. Practice Generosity

Generosity is an important aspect of building generational wealth. It is the willingness to share what you have with others, whether it is your time, money, or resources. By practicing generosity, you can build a sense of community and support that can help you achieve your financial goals. It also helps to develop a sense of gratitude and abundance, which is essential for cultivating a prosperous mindset.

5. Focus on Education and Knowledge

Education and knowledge are key components of building generational wealth. It is important to develop a deep understanding of financial principles and to stay up-to-date on the latest trends and developments. This requires a commitment to lifelong learning and a willingness to invest in your education. By focusing on education and knowledge, you can develop the skills and expertise necessary to build wealth over the long term.

6. Seek Guidance from Mentors

Finally, seeking guidance from mentors is an essential strategy for building generational wealth. Mentors can provide valuable insight, advice, and support as you navigate the complexities of building wealth over the long term. They can help you avoid common pitfalls and develop a mindset that is focused on long-term success. By seeking guidance from mentors, you can accelerate your progress and build wealth more quickly than you would on your own.

Building generational wealth requires a mindset that is focused on long-term success, discipline, and intentionality. It requires a commitment to developing good money habits, cultivating a culture of financial responsibility, and practicing generosity. It also requires a willingness to invest in education and seek guidance from mentors. By adopting these strategies, you can develop a prosperous mindset that can help you build generational wealth and create a legacy that can be passed on to future generations.

Tips for Passing on Financial Mindset to Future Generations

Creating generational wealth requires not just a focus on money and financial strategies but also on developing a healthy and prosperous mindset around money. Passing on this mindset to future generations is essential in creating a legacy of financial success. In this chapter, we will discuss tips for passing on a healthy financial mindset to your children and grandchildren.

1. Start Early: It is never too early to start teaching your children about financial responsibility. Even young children can understand the concept of earning and saving money. Encourage them to save a portion of their allowance or earnings from chores, and help them set goals for what they want to use the money for. This helps them understand the value of money and the importance of saving for the future.

2. Lead by Example: Children often learn by watching their parents, so it is important to lead by example. Practice what you preach and model healthy financial habits, such as budgeting, saving, and investing. This not only helps your children learn about financial responsibility but also creates a positive association with money and success.

3. Teach the Value of Hard Work: It is important to instill the value of hard work in children. Encourage them to work hard and set goals for themselves, and reward them for their achievements. This teaches them the importance of effort and dedication in achieving financial success.

4. Emphasize the Importance of Education: Education is one of the most powerful tools in creating financial success. Encourage your children to pursue education and learning, and help them understand how education can lead to higher income and more opportunities for financial prosperity.

5. Teach the Power of Giving: It is important to teach children about the power of giving back. This can be in the form of charitable donations or volunteer work. When children understand the

importance of giving, they are more likely to develop a mindset of abundance and generosity, which can lead to greater financial success.

6. Encourage Entrepreneurship: Entrepreneurship is a great way to cultivate a mindset of financial independence and prosperity. Encourage your children to explore their interests and talents and to think creatively about how they can turn those into a business or career. This can help them develop an entrepreneurial spirit and a mindset of abundance and success.

7. Teach the Importance of Delayed Gratification: Delayed gratification is the ability to resist the temptation of immediate rewards in order to achieve greater rewards in the future. This is a key skill in achieving financial success. Teach your children about the importance of delayed gratification, and help them understand the long-term benefits of saving and investing for the future.

8. Encourage a Growth Mindset: A growth mindset is the belief that abilities and skills can be developed through hard work and dedication. Encourage your children to have a growth mindset when it comes to their financial success. Help them understand that with hard work, dedication, and a positive attitude, they can achieve anything they set their minds to.

9. Foster a Mindset of Gratitude: Gratitude is a powerful tool in creating a prosperous mindset. Encourage your children to focus on the positive aspects of their lives, and to be grateful for what they have. This can help them develop a mindset of abundance and attract greater financial success.

Passing on a healthy financial mindset to future generations is essential in creating a legacy of financial success. By starting early, leading by example, emphasizing the importance of education and hard work, and fostering a mindset of gratitude and abundance, you can help your children and grandchildren achieve their financial goals and create a prosperous future for themselves and their families.

Conclusion

Throughout this guide, we have explored the various aspects of cultivating a prosperous and healthy mindset for financial success. We have learned that money is more than just a tool for acquiring material possessions; it is a means for achieving greater peace of mind, freedom, and security.

We began by examining the connection between mindset and financial success, emphasizing the importance of developing a positive and resilient attitude towards money. We delved into the role of self-care, forgiveness, and spirituality in promoting financial well-being, highlighting the benefits of prioritizing these practices in our daily lives.

We explored strategies for overcoming financial setbacks and building financial resilience, recognizing that these challenges are an inevitable part of the journey towards financial independence. By reframing our mindset towards these setbacks, we can use them as opportunities for growth and learning.

We also recognized the importance of passing on these healthy financial habits to future generations, recognizing that true generational wealth is not just about financial assets but also about the attitudes and values we instill in our children and grandchildren.

Finally, we offered practical tips and techniques for incorporating these strategies into our daily lives, recognizing that lasting change requires consistent effort and dedication.

In conclusion, the journey towards financial prosperity is not just about acquiring wealth; it is about cultivating a mindset that allows us to live a life of abundance and fulfillment. By prioritizing self-care, forgiveness, spirituality, and a positive attitude towards money, we can create a life of purpose and meaning that transcends material possessions. May you embark on this journey with grace, courage, and a heart full of gratitude.

As we come to the end of this journey, I want to express my deepest gratitude to you for taking the time to read through this material. It is my sincere hope that the wisdom and insights shared here have been of great value to you in your pursuit of financial abundance and freedom.

I humbly ask that you consider leaving a positive review of this work. Your feedback will help to spread the message and inspire others to embark on their own journeys towards financial prosperity.

May you continue to cultivate a prosperous mindset and experience abundance in all areas of your life.

Thank you for your time and attention.